To M...

CW00557604

essential
elvisinterviews

THANKS FOR HELPING TO KEEP
THE KING REMEMBERED.

ENJOY!

Copyright © 2005 by Andrew Hearn

First published in Great Britain in 2005 by
ESSENTIAL ELVIS UK
PO Box 4176
Worthing
W. Sussex
BN14 9DW
www.essentialelvis.com

ISBN: 0-9549820-0-2

A CIP catalogue record for this book is
available from the British Library.

Cover photograph: © Tom Salva
Back cover photograph: © Russ Howe

Cover design by Andrew Hearn

Interviews by Andrew Hearn for Essential Elvis
magazine. All interviews (except with Bill Belew and
Suzanna Leigh) are re-printed from Essential Elvis
magazine where they originally appeared.
All others used with permission.

No attempt has been made by the interviewer / author
to modify or edit any part of the interview. Remarks
and opinions remain those of the interviewee, not the
interviewer, author or Essential Elvis magazine.

Layout by Julie Mundy
www.julie.mundy.com

Acknowledgments

Elvis A. Presley
The most ordinary extraordinary man

This book is dedicated to the subject matter, whose music and influence has been a part of everyday life for as long as I can remember. Also, to the memory of my mother, Sylvia Ann Goldsmith, a dedicated Elvis fan who ensured a safe and loving upbringing.

I'd like to thank several people who made this book possible. Tom Salva and Russ Howe for pushing me to achieve such results. Julie Mundy for being such a supportive friend over so many years, and Diane Johnston; the only person I know to have actually worn one of Elvis' original jumpsuits - and looked as good.

I'd also like to express my appreciation and respect to all of the people interviewed, many of which have become close friends.

And to my wife Polly and baby son Toby. Thank you both for your unconditional love and support... And for your toleration to my Elvis obsession!

Toby enjoys his first trip to Graceland. January 2004

Contents

40. FRANCINE YORK
Actress who appeared with Elvis in the movie *Tickle Me*
First appeared in issue 10 - May / June 2000

45. HARRY HILL
British comedian, TV personality and Elvis fan
First appeared in issue 11 - July / Aug 2000

50. DEBORAH WALLEY
Elvis' co-star in *Spinout*
First appeared in issue 13 - Nov / Dec 2000

54. RICK SCHMIDLIN
Producer of *Elvis: That's The Way It Is* - Special Edition
First appeared in issue 13 - Nov / Dec 2000

58. SONNY WEST
Long-term friend, bodyguard and member of Elvis' inner circle
First appeared in issue 14 - Jan / Feb 2000

68. LIONEL HUDSON
Who appeared in the original movie *Elvis: That's The Way It Is*
First appeared in issue 14 - Jan / Feb 2000

72. ANITA WOOD
Elvis' sweetheart from the 1950s
First appeared in issue 15 - March / April 2001

77. MARC BANNERMAN
EastEnders actor and Elvis fan
First appeared in issue 15 - March / April 2001

83. LINDA THOMPSON
Elvis' girlfriend and companion 1972-76
First appeared in issue 17 - July / Aug 2001

Foreword

Hello readers,

I am John Wilkinson. From mid-1968 until that tragic day of August 16th 1977, I had the pleasure and honour of being Elvis Presley's rhythm guitar player in his famed TCB Band. In all of my 44 years of being in show business, those nine and a half years were the most exciting, memorable and fun.

The book that you are holding in your hands is destined to be one of the most important and informative of all your collection. The Elvis myth and mystique has been carried on by many fan clubs all over the world, this book comes to the public by way of one of the largest and most influential organisations dedicated to the music and memory of Elvis. The magazine is aptly named *Essential Elvis*.

Andrew Hearn, as the editor and publisher, brings Elvis to you through the eyes of a fan. Over the years, Mr. Hearn has met with, and interviewed, many of Elvis' closest friends, members of his stage show production, relatives and fans. As one of those people that did work closely with Elvis, and was considered to be a close friend, I would say that this book brings to you the Elvis that I knew. He was a haunted yet optimistic man; a man that gave all that he had or could give to his fans, and sometimes, complete strangers.

This book brings to you the Elvis that desperately wanted to be just one of the guys, but couldn't be because he was trapped by his amazing fame.

I'm so happy that Andrew Hearn has asked me to write a little something for his new book. It's truly an honour for me. Now my friends, get ready to get to know the greatest entertainer the world has ever known: Elvis Presley.

May all your dreams come true,

John Wilkinson

Introduction

Talk About The Good Times

It is with sincere appreciation that I thank you for purchasing this unique book. Being the editor and publisher of the UK's official Elvis Presley magazine really has to be one of the most rewarding jobs in terms of personal fulfilment. Since Elvis burst onto the scene in the mid-1950s, there has been no shortage of rumours and half-truths surrounding his private life. Fortunately, in an effort to discover his true personality, my position has allowed me to talk to the people who were actually there, alongside the man who changed all of our lives.

Since launching *Essential Elvis* over ten years ago, there has been an incredible amount of memorable moments; most of which involve meeting and interviewing many of the King's closest friends, associates and celebrity fans.

With a steadily growing reputation as being the Elvis publication that produces the most unique interviews, it had become an ambition to publish a book to offer an interesting collection of some of our best features. Within these pages you'll enjoy over thirty personal recollections illustrated with many unseen photographs from the archives of collector Russ Howe. With guest contributors including Julie Mundy and Diane Johnston, this book will allow you to experience the rollercoaster that was life alongside one of the most influential figures of the twentieth century.

Several of the familiar names included actually granted *Essential Elvis* their only fan-based magazine interview. Their memories have been exclusively shared with us and some incredible secrets have been disclosed for the very first time.

In a world of litigation and prenuptial agreements, it will not come as a surprise to learn that some of the interviews featured were conducted under pre-agreed terms. Out of consideration and respect, some of the delicate subject matters surrounding Elvis' private life were omitted from our questioning at the interviewees request. No doubt, reviewers will perceive this as missed opportunities; however, some of the more controversial interviews would've undoubtedly been declined altogether without such understanding.

The selection of unedited transcripts presented in this exciting book will surely not disappoint. Even the world's most hardcore fans will savour such incredible stories, guaranteed to bring you a new and refreshing insight into the private life of Elvis Presley.

Andrew Hearn
Editor & publisher, Essential Elvis
The UK's official Elvis Presley magazine
email: editor@essentialelvis.com

" My heart was beating so fast I was afraid he could hear it. **"**

Julie Parrish

Julie's professional acting career began as a result of winning a national contest for 'Young Model of the Year' at a modelling school chain. First prize was an appearance in Jerry Lewis' *It's Only Money* (1962), billed as Joyce Wilbar. She changed her name to Julie Parrish just before making her second film, *The Nutty Professor*, again with Jerry Lewis, in 1963.

Julie made many guest appearances on TV series, including *Dobie Gillis*, before taking that memorable helicopter ride with Elvis Presley in *Paradise, Hawaiian Style*. Julie played Joanna, the girl who works at the Kahala Hilton. She also had the distinction of being in the scene where Elvis sings *A Dog's Life*, which definitely ranks amongst the most embarrassing of Elvis' movie songs.

Julie went on to appear as Miss Piper in an episode of *Star Trek: The Menagerie*, which used footage from the original un-aired pilot episode, *The Cage*. More recently, Julie played Maggie Brady in the TV series, *Capitol*.

Before her unfortunate death from cancer on October 1st 2003, Julie was a full-time counsellor at Haven Hills shelter for battered women and their children. She spoke out openly against domestic violence whenever she could, especially to teens. On top of all that, she landed the recurring role of Joan Diamond on the TV series, *Beverly Hills 90210*, which she somehow squeezed into her busy schedule. She also enjoyed attending Elvis conventions throughout the USA, including several events in Memphis.

Firstly Julie, how did you get the part in *Paradise, Hawaiian Style*?
My agent set up an audition for me. I was one of the women selected to do a screen test for the role of Joanna, but I didn't get the part at first. I really wanted to work with Elvis, and I was upset by what I considered a lack of direction on the part of the director.

I asked my agent to get me another chance, but he couldn't convince them to give me another test. He told me that there was this nothing part to be used in the titles of an upcoming film called *Boeing, Boeing* for which I could audition and in that way get back into the office of the same producer, Mr. Hal Wallis, in order to state my case. My agent added that if I was selected for the bit part, I would have to do it, otherwise my credibility (probably his too) would be questioned. The part in *Boeing, Boeing* was embarrassing. It was just a shot where I am this woman walking along a street in France who gets her bottom pinched by some guy, but I wanted to work with Elvis!

So, I went to the audition, convinced the producer to re-test me and had to do the embarrassing role as well. My friends were appalled. One friend offered to pay me not to do it. Fortunately, the part in *Boeing, Boeing* was cut out, although I did have the film on my resume for a while. My agent had me include it, because I didn't have a lot of credits at that time. However, somewhere out there in the world *Boeing, Boeing* is still on a list of credits attributed to me, because every now and then I get a fan letter from someone requesting an autograph who, among other bits of flattery, tells me how great I was in the film. I never know whether to point out to the person that I wasn't in the film, or to let it go and just say, thank you.

Can you recall your first meeting with Elvis?

I was very nervous. I had been in every Elvis Presley fan club I could find when I was a kid. He was the only star that I ever entered a fan club for. I did my Elvis impressions in front of the student body at assembly time at school and anywhere else where someone would watch me. So, there I was, a few years later, standing in front of him trying to seem, I'm sure, like I did this sort of thing everyday. I didn't actually meet him until we were on the set, and he was very polite and sweet to me. We made some small talk, and I got through it. I'd like to do a hypnotic regression someday to re-create for myself what actually transpired because it's a bit of a blur now. I think we talked a little about the scene we were doing. His so-called Memphis Mafia was around to distract him between takes, so I didn't actually hang out with Elvis ever. It almost seemed set up that way. That was their job. We just did the scenes, joked around a little and that was usually it. At that time in my life I had 'authority figure' fears, stemming from my upbringing, and I would usually shy away from intimate conversation with someone I was in awe of, so the guys would have had nothing to worry about if they were concerned that I was going to make a move on Elvis.

"*Elvis would have been another James Dean.***"**

What were your first impressions?

Elvis seemed shy, and he was so handsome he took my breath away. My heart was beating so fast I was afraid he could hear it. He had a twinkle in his eye and joked around a bit. He seemed kind and caring and a little nervous at meeting someone new. He did not seem all that comfortable with me at first, but then I was not all that comfortable with him either, to say the least.

Did you think he enjoyed doing the movie?

He did not express his feelings to me personally so I don't really know. I got the feeling that he was just getting through it, but was being responsible and professional and doing as good a job he could with what he had to work with. I know he didn't like the song he had to sing to me, and certainly the script and story line were uninspired.

As an actor he was so much more than the parts given to him in those Hal Wallis movies. That was obvious in his first films. He was just great in *King Creole, Jailhouse Rock* and even in *Love Me Tender*.

I think he did a great job considering it was his very first film. He could have gone so far with his acting. I think he would have been another James Dean.

What did you all do off set?

I didn't really see Elvis off the set.

What did Elvis talk about? What was he into at the time?

He was into metaphysical studies. He talked about spirituality.

Everyone knows Elvis loved animals. How did you get on with that famous

helicopter scene with all those dogs?
It was actually a lot of fun. The dogs were well trained, but being confined in that cramped space for such a long time because of having to do the scene over and over to get things right from all angles, must have been confusing and a real bore to them. Elvis played with them between takes. He talked to the dogs and petted them a lot. They liked him; it was obvious.

When we did that scene, I had just gotten out of the hospital and Hal Wallis sat in his tall chair on the set nearby watching all through the shooting of it. I'm not sure why he was doing that, but it made things a bit uncomfortable. Mr. Wallis, a married man, was an old letch and was constantly calling me and asking me out while we were on location. I never went out with him, but it was the 1960s and we were told not to hurt someone's feelings at all costs when they were in a position to hire you. I constantly made excuses to him. It was quite annoying and insulting actually. I dreaded his daily calls. I think he felt it was an unspoken promise that I would sleep with him since he had allowed me to re-test for the part. There was a day before the film started that he called me into his office, locked the door behind us, led me over to the sofa and briefly kissed me on the mouth. He said, "Little girl, we're going to have a long talk about your future." I looked at my watch and apologised saying I'd like to stay and talk but that I really had an audition I had to get to.

On his last call to me on location in Hawaii, he said to me, "Little girl, you'd better think again," and I knew I would probably never work for him again, but that was just fine with me. He was old enough to be my grandfather and quite ugly as well. Being practically a child and pretty plastic in my choices, I was highly offended. I'm not claiming to have been an innocent babe, but when I make mistakes, I like for them to be due to a choice of my own. I think the stress of all this nonsense contributed to my becoming ill during that film. One day on the set, when we were doing the scene where all the girls converge on Elvis to confront him about dating all of us at the same time while using us to promote his helicopter business, I began to have pain in my right leg. The scene involved the production number with the song *You're Gonna Get What You're Lookin' For....* or second thoughts maybe it was called *Stop Where You Are.* I forget, but I remember thinking it was the best song in the film. We had to do the scene so very many times over and over and I was standing in high-heeled shoes. Suddenly, there was a pain in the whole right side of my body and I complained of it and had to sit down. Elvis came over, picked me up in his arms and carried me to his dressing room and laid me down on his sofa. He then tried to do a healing. He held his hands about a foot above my body for a while, but I was so nervous worrying about what everyone on the set must be thinking that I couldn't enjoy it.

How stupid of me, I think now. I told Elvis I thought we ought to go back to the set. Anyway, we finished the scene and when we returned to the mainland, I went into the hospital for tests. It was thought that I might have had a slight stroke, but my intuition told me that it had to do with taking Librium, diet pills and drinking alcohol. We didn't know the dangers then. It was customary that after a day's shooting the crew and some of the actors, not Elvis, would go to dinner at the club in the hotel, and there would always be drinking. After that experience, I never took another diet pill again. I had been also been taking tranquillisers since the age of fourteen. I never took another of those either. It was a voice inside me that told me not to, not a doctor. The whole experience scared me.

Wow, incredible stuff. I hear Elvis wasn't too keen on that annoying kid Donna Butterworth right?
If this was so, he never mentioned it to me. She was precocious, but I quite enjoyed her.

Did you get involved with any pranks with Elvis or the guys?
I don't remember any pranks, but that may be because it was so long ago. The guys were all very nice to me, and they were very respectful. That's all I remember.

Did Elvis give you any gifts?
He sent me beautiful flowers.

The girls want to know what it was like to kiss Elvis.
He had very soft lips. Being in his arms was almost scary to me.

And finally Julie, how should the world remember Elvis Presley?

The world should remember Elvis as a kind and generous man who cared. He didn't publicise his donations to help others because he didn't do it for the accolades. He should be remembered as a man whose music basically changed the world, the culture, everything. It made the young people of the day be a force to be reckoned with. Before that, they didn't have much of a voice. After Elvis came on the scene, they had some kind of power.

❝ If Elvis didn't think he had done a song that was at its absolute maximum best, he'd be willing to go on and do thirty more takes. **❞**

Mike Stoller

Could you tell us how you first met Elvis Presley?

Well, the first time Jerry and I met Elvis was in a recording studio; it was Radio Recorders in Hollywood. It was actually a studio that we knew well because it was the same one in which we recorded Big Mama Thornton's *Hound Dog* in 1952. By the time we actually met Elvis he had already recorded three or four songs of ours, he'd done *Hound Dog* of course, which was a cover and *Love Me*, which was originally a duet by Willie & Ruth on our own label called Spark Records. We were told that Elvis had

requested us to be at the studio, he knew our songs and he knew that we made good records.

So, we were invited to be there and although we were not given the title of producers, that's in effect what we did. The actual supervisor was a guy named Steve Sholes who worked for RCA but what Steve did at the time, more or less, was to recite a master number take one, take two and so on.

So what were your first impressions?

He was great. He was a very shy young man and he really wasn't that much younger than us, just a couple of years I guess. We got along great, fooling around you know, playing different things at the piano and so on.

Did he come across as professional as others have said?
Oh, he was very professional and not only that, he had great, great stamina. If he didn't think he had done a song that was at its absolute maximum best, he'd be willing to go on and do thirty more takes. I remember *Jailhouse Rock* for example, Jerry and I knew that we had a great take at around take 7, 8 or 9 and he just went on up into the high twenties thinking he could always do one better. And then we all came back, sat around and listened, he agreed that the earlier take was the best.

Fans can see you playing the piano in the movie *Jailhouse Rock*.
Actually, they asked Jerry to play in the movie and he explained that he wasn't a piano player and they said that it's all right 'cos you look like one. It was all pre-recorded, so when it came to it you just moved your fingers across the keys so it just looked like you were playing the piano. Anyway, the day that the filming started Jerry had a terrible toothache and he called and asked me to go and cover for him. I said that the producer would be very upset because they wanted him, but he said that they wouldn't even know the difference. I went in and they told me to shave my beard off, as it was a scene-stealer, so I took the beard off and I'm the fella in the film.

Did you witness the shooting of the famous *Jailhouse Rock* scene?
No, sadly I wasn't there when they shot the dance number.

Can you tell us about Judy Tyler?
Well, she was a very, very nice girl and she'd actually come from Broadway in which she starred in various musicals. She had just got married on July 4th, which is our big holiday and she was with her husband up in Utah somewhere, and she died in an automobile accident.

I wasn't with Elvis when the news came through because the filming itself was completed. It was probably sometime around late May, early June when we finished filming and the accident was in July. We heard about it on the radio but I didn't see Elvis after that until the next film, which was the last one that we were really involved in, it was *King Creole* of course.

Were you lucky enough to spend any time at Graceland during the early years?
The first time I was in Graceland, Jerry and I, was two years ago. It was the first time we'd even been to Memphis too, but it kinda' has happened to us before. We wrote *Kansas City* in 1952 and the first time we were over there was 1986 (laughs) when they gave us the key to the city.

Do you still keep in touch with people such as Scotty Moore and DJ Fontana who you worked with in the studio and on the film set?
I can't say that we really stayed in touch, but I did see them and it was great. It was at the big Elvis tribute in Memphis and it was the first time I saw them live. It was so nice to shake hands after all those years.

Scotty Moore is known as a very shy man who doesn't say a lot. How was he back then?
He was always like that. He was very quiet, a nice player and very even-tempered. I guess he must've got pretty angry at times but he always kept it inside.

I met Scotty a few years back and he has bad arthritis and It's hard for him to play nowadays.
Oh my, that's very sad. I bet he can still knock out a good tune, DJ can certainly whack away at those drums. It was great to see these guys at this event. Of course, Bill Black died a long time ago, I think it was the early 1960s.

Are you still proud of the album *Elvis Sings Leiber & Stoller*. Do you have a copy?
Oh yes, I do have a copy and it came out on CD as well. When it came out on CD I was delighted to find there was a song that we had submitted for a film all those years ago. We actually wrote it for the movie *Love In Las Vegas (Viva Las Vegas)*. I thought they just didn't like it and so it wasn't used. It turned out that they did record it; they just didn't use it in the film. It was a duet with Ann Margret and it's called *You're The Boss*. So, the first time I'd even heard it was on the CD *Elvis Sings Leiber & Stoller*.

What's the nicest memory you have of Elvis? What sticks in your mind the most?
I have a few, but one in particular was on the set of *Jailhouse Rock*. One day he said to me, "Mike, I would like you to write me a real pretty ballad." and that was on a Friday. We didn't usually work weekends but on the Saturday Jerry and I wrote a song called *Don't* and on Sunday we took it to a fella named Young Jesse who sometimes performed along with The Coasters, and we made a demo. I gave it to him on the Monday and he loved it, but there was a bit of a problem because it hadn't gone through the proper channels, they didn't want anybody giving Elvis anything directly. The Colonel and our boss tried to control everything, but if Elvis really loved something he'd do it, it was to do with publishing rights.

I don't think there's anyone who doesn't know that wonderful song. What a great memory.
Why, thank you.

I could probably talk to you all day, but I know you're preparing to catch a flight. I must finally ask you how you think people should remember Elvis Presley?
In my view, I think they should remember the dynamic young man, he really was. He had a gift, no question about it. It's best to remember him that way rather than later on when he became troubled.

Thanks for your time and have a safe trip back to California this afternoon Mike.
It's a pleasure.

" Each moment was so intense that we totally loved each other. "

Jennifer Holden

Everybody remembers the stubborn blonde Sherry Wilson who gave Vince Everett a hard time in the 1957 movie *Jailhouse Rock*. Things on the set were much the same to begin with...

Hi Jennifer, is it a good time to call?
Oh yeah, I just got in, but I'd like to interview you if you don't mind, just for a change.

Okay, go ahead.
How long have you been involved in the Elvis thing?

I've had the magazine for about six years now, but the colour edition was launched just a few months ago, so it's pretty much a new thing. It's snowballed into something quite big though.
That's amazing.
Are you a computer person?

Well, a little bit, but anyway, I've a few questions for you. I'm going to start with a couple of obvious ones. Tell us how you got the part in *Jailhouse Rock*.
Well, I was in a movie previously to that with Robert Taylor called *Tipping A Dead Jockey* and these were *Rebel Without A Cause*-type people. I couldn't seem to

walk ten steps and say what I was supposed to say. I kind of said what I felt like and although the director liked it, Robert Taylor almost had a heart attack. The director promised me I'd be in his next film and that was it. It turned out to be *Jailhouse Rock*.

Do you remember your very first meeting with Elvis? Who put you two together?
It was back in Vegas and I was introduced to him when he was playing at the Frontier. He looked really bad back then, wearing an old leather jacket and I thought I'd just stick my foot out and trip him as he walked by. Some friends of mine did introduce us, but I didn't really get to know him until I did the film.

When you finally did get together for the film, did you get on from day one?
We got along great but at first it was a little tricky because I think he was going through a lot of emotional changes because he knew he was going to be drafted. Usually when you come on set you're introduced to your co-stars and everybody really tries to make everyone else feel really comfortable. Elvis just sat in one corner with his boys. Once we got acquainted properly we did become really good friends.

Elvis loved the ladies, as we all know. Did he flirt with you at all?
Okay, the director bought up the lovemaking scene right? And we still felt pretty cold towards each other and you can see that in my face. Well, we had to do the kissing part and I remember thinking that I was going to give it all I had to break his shell. It went quite well and I broke down his defences and there weren't many takes as it worked so well.

Did you socialise with Elvis off set?
No, not as such. After we did the pool scene I went back to my dressing room and there was a faulty switch. I went to pull the cord by the door and all of a sudden this flame fired at me, it was pouring out of the socket. I was so scared that I shouted for Elvis and so he came running back and pushed the door open and then he invited me to dinner and we talked a lot about the problems he was having. He was very deeply insecure about what was going to happen to him with the army thing; it was just around the corner.

Was there any fooling around with the boys?
Not really, he just hung out with the guys and that was it. I do actually remember the guys, but I never really kept in touch with any of them.

Now here's a question for you. It's puzzled many fans and it's had me wondering too. The pool scene was obviously filmed on a hot summer's day as everyone wore short-sleeved shirts or bikinis. During the performance of *Baby, I Don't Care* however, Elvis is baking in a high-necked woollen jumper. Any idea why?
It certainly wasn't cold, a typical Californian day. But it was probably how they dressed him. The wardrobe person knew exactly how they wanted him to look. I mean, I was never too crazy about the make-up they put us in anyway. At the time we were shooting the film we had to look typical of the people there in Hollywood.

Did you have any indication then of just how long Elvis would last?
Did you realise that he'd still be as popular as he is today?
The night we went out we had a conversation where I told him that he'd never have anything to worry about and that his big concern was that nobody was ever going to say no to him and yes, I knew he'd be big.

What about romance, was there any?
You see, when we were acting together we were in love. If an actor can't take it to that depth then nobody can believe

them so each moment was so intense that we totally loved each other. It made a good film because it was totally believable.

It's a hard question but is there anything in particular that stands out in your mind. Did Elvis do or say anything that you recall more than anything else?
Yeah, it is a hard one because everything that we said was very heavy duty, even when we weren't getting along. It was so intense when we did it and when we were on film I even made things up so it was so off-the-wall. I mean, when we kissed and I said that I was coming all unglued, it was just an ad-lib.

That's wonderful, I bet fans will look out for that part with interest next time they watch the movie.

Well, this leads me to the inevitable question; how do you think the world should remember Elvis Presley?
I think that he actually bought black music to the world when the white man couldn't accept it. He literally introduced it even though Little Richard was on the scene. I myself loved blues and I was raised on it in Chicago. Because he bought it out, he set off everybody from the Beatles to the Rolling Stones and everyone else.

Well, thanks for the chat Jennifer, I'm hoping to persuade you to come over to England as a guest at one of our events by the way.
I've never been to England, isn't that awful. I'd love to come, thanks for phoning.

" We were all growing boys enjoying ourselves, it was all wine, women and song. "

Lamar Fike

Lamar, how are you enjoying the summer?
Pretty Good, it's burning blazes here. How are you?

It's warm, but not as warm as your part of the world I guess.
Well, you only get about 80°C there but a good place to spend your summer is in Finland.

Do you spend a lot of time in Europe?
Yes, I do.

Well, I'm really grateful for your time Lamar.
Let me tell you something. Whatever you need, just make that call.

Okay, let's start at the beginning. How did you actually meet Elvis? Didn't you hang around the Graceland gates so much that you both finally became friends?
No, absolutely not. Cliff Gleaves first introduced him to me, but I actually first met him properly in 1954, Sam Phillips introduced us at Sun Records. I saw him again after he'd just done *Blue Moon* and you know we just became friends. Elvis said, "Why don't you come up to the house?" and so Cliff Gleaves took me up there a couple of times and I stayed with him ever since then. That's how it happened; I never hung around any gates in my life.

So what was your connection with Sam Phillips?
Well, I always wanted to be a disc jockey and Sam taught me some stuff. I'd just be hanging around Sun Studios and stuff like that because I liked the black artists. So yeah, it was Sam that really introduced me to Elvis back in 1954 during one of his recording sessions there.

We have an image of just Elvis, Scotty, Bill and Sam Phillips. Was the place always full of people?
Yeah, sort of. People were hanging around quite a bit you know. It was like the beginning of everything back then and it eventually became Memphis really.

Apart from Graceland itself, Sun Studio is the place that's guaranteed to put a shiver down your spine.
Oh yeah, the Circle G ranch out in Mississippi is pretty special too. You wouldn't believe that place; it's like a time warp there. Elvis bought that ranch so he could eventually retire there. He really wanted to move there and set up home there and he was going to put a place there for all of us too.

Surely this wouldn't have been instead of Graceland?
He would have eventually moved out of Graceland. I'm not saying he didn't love Graceland, but he just loved that ranch. He loved the acreage and he loved all that room. He wanted to build a new house for himself and one for each of us.

So, if this really was to happen, what would've happened to Graceland do you think?
He would've certainly kept Graceland. I don't think he would've ever sold it and he would've had both places so he could go back and forth.

When you first started to go up to Graceland, what was Vernon and Gladys like? Was their relationship a little stormy?

I think that the term 'stormy' doesn't quite cut it. Gladys really sort of ran the family and you know, Vernon had a permanent backache for 30 years, so Gladys really was the leader of the household. As soon as Elvis was born he became close to her and this was part of the phone calls and all. Elvis would be checking on her and making the best of a bad situation, but he called home all the time to make sure Vernon hadn't beat up on her. Elvis was always kind to his father but you're right, it was a strained relationship.

Was this whilst on the road or in the army?

He always called. Whether it was on tour or in the army, but Gladys was dead by then.

Elvis had a lot of girls in the army didn't he, especially whilst on leave in Paris?

That's an understatement! When we went into town it would literally be tons (laughs) because we were all growing boys enjoying ourselves, it was all wine, women and song. There were lovely girls at the Lido in Paris and some were Bluebell Girls from England actually. They were nice girls and very pretty too. We enjoyed their company.

Remember the Hollywood parties in the '60s? What kind of people would you see there?

They weren't really parties. Everyone would just get together and have some fun and shoot pool and stuff. They were gatherings rather than parties.

Did you ever see Dean Martin at one of these gatherings?

No, never.

What about our old friend PJ Proby? He tells us he knew Elvis and the Colonel really well.

Yeah, I know PJ. He did meet Elvis a couple of times, but I wouldn't describe them as real good buddies. But I know him and he's a pretty good guy.

He played Elvis in the West End musical some time back. It's funny that a guy of his age was portraying Elvis during the Las Vegas comeback. Elvis would've been in his mid-30s then.

Well I'm sixty-three so I'd say he must be about sixty-four years old now. We did a copy of that play in Finland with a guy who lives in Cheltenham.

Clayton Marks?

You know him? He's a sweetheart, a real nice person. He married a lovely girl named Jackie and he has two beautiful children. He still works a lot in Europe.

I've got to ask. Do you remember Elvis giving you your TCB pendant?

Oh certainly. I was given one of the first few TCBs ever made and I still have it. A jeweller firm in Beverly Hills made it. The presentations weren't really a big thing. He just said, "Here, I got something for you." and that was it. Elvis didn't make a big thing out of it because after a while, when you gave away as much as he had over a period of years, it almost became normal. I've still got my bracelet too.

What's the nickname engraved on it?

Great Speckled Bird is on the back of it.

I don't want to sound rude, but you were often the butt of a few Elvis jokes.

Oh every day. He knew were he stood with me and it was like water off a duck's back. Elvis and I were so close and I used to give him what I thought. Whenever I got ready to talk he'd always listen and sometimes he'd ask everyone about the show then he'd come to me and say, "I just don't want to hear it." and I'd say, "Okay."

I think fans would be disappointed if I didn't ask you about the Goldman book.

The research for that thing was done in

1978 and you'd think that after a while somebody would let up on that. You're talking over thirty years ago and people must be tired of talking about it. I really didn't like the book, but that was the style of a guy like Albert Goldman. It wasn't a case of twisting anything I said, but he put it together the way he wanted to. It was just the way Albert wrote and he really didn't care about what people thought of him. I don't speak ill of the dead and he's dead, that's the end of it.

We know now that RCA would record shows throughout the 1970s. Apparently anyone could ask the sound engineer for a copy and it was yours.
I can honestly tell you that I was never sure of that, but the engineer was Bill Porter. What I see and hear in bootlegging is that there was a lot of people recording a lot of stuff. I don't have any unreleased shows or anything because we didn't have to worry about the product because we had the real thing.

I recently came across a fantastic photograph of you bounding on stage with Elvis on your back. Even more strange is that if you look closely at the photograph, Elvis has a stuffed gorilla on his back. What was going on there?
Yeah, I remember that night. He just jumped on my back and I was walking around with him backstage. We had fun with it and I walked out on stage with him there on my back. We are the living link to Elvis and we will be until we die and I'm proud of that. Elvis would get totally insane and there was something going on all the time. Elvis and I were argumentative; I'd be up there in the balcony doing the lights at a show and he and I would start arguing with each other. He'd accuse me of not doing this and that and he'd say, "I hope you remember to turn the lights off." and so I did. It'd go dark and he'd say, "Okay, I'm sorry" and I'd turn them back on. It was so funny that it got to be a routine that we'd use in the show.

> *"Elvis hated Vegas, he hated Vegas so much you have no idea. He didn't want to live with it because it was do it or die."*

What about the show in February 1973 when the drunken guys stormed on stage to attack Elvis? What really went on that night?
It wasn't as great as Elvis made it out to be. They jumped on stage but they really didn't know what they were doing. Elvis sort of reacted very strongly by knocking one of them down with karate and then Red got them off the stage. The whole thing was so spur-of-the-moment and all of a sudden it's on you, but Elvis was always prepared and who isn't in that arena? Things like that would happen, but Elvis got a little carried away with it.

What about the whole Las Vegas thing? Was Elvis really interested in performing there during the last few years of his life?
He hated Vegas, he hated Vegas so much you have no idea. He just got tired of it; he was just totally worn out. He didn't want to live with it because it was do it or die. He hated it. I think Vegas helped him die. It really caused him a lot of problems. You can't do a show like Elvis did for four solid weeks; three or four shows a night. Nobody in the world does that. It's a fact that Vegas contributed to his death.

It's a direct question Lamar; how do you think Elvis died?
I think he died of terminal apathy.

We all know drugs contributed to Elvis' death, but do you think they caused it?
Sure they did.

But it was a heart attack?
You know, somebody said that the guy who steps in front of a lorry and the last thing he sees is that thing. I'm sure he had a heart attack before he died. He fell over and suffocated and this causes heart attacks.

Where were you at the time Lamar?
I was in Portland getting ready for the tour. They called me and I flew straight back in to Memphis. It was the worst thing that's ever happened to me.

I don't want to dwell on that stuff too much so...
That's okay Andrew. You give me questions and I'll give you answers. Elvis used to say, "Don't ask Lamar anything 'cause you'll get an answer!"

We'd love to have you over to the UK sometime Lamar.
I'd love to come over later on in the year?

Sounds great.
What else is going on Bud?

Well, it's the calm before the storm at the moment. With Elvis Week just around the corner it's all going to start going crazy, in Memphis and here too.
I think the big one will be in a couple of years, the twenty-fifth anniversary.

Me too. Do you still see Red and Sonny?
Oh yeah, I see Red all the time. Marty is a super guy but people misunderstand him, he's kind of a bit like me, a straight shooter and he doesn't mix words.

Marty and I are in touch regularly and that's really nice to hear.
Well Andrew, I may see you pretty soon.

I hope so Lamar, thanks again.
Pleasure.

" Even today people ask to shake the hand that shook the King's. "

Sir Jimmy Saville OBE

Sir Jim, fans will be aware of several well-published photos of you and Elvis on the set of *Roustabout*. How did the meeting come about and were you in America just to see Elvis?
Yes and no really. I went as a DJ for Radio Luxembourg to meet up with various artists like the Everly Brothers etc. Elvis was my biggest goal of course.

Elvis looks great in those photos although lots of people say he didn't photograph well. I've been told several times that he was far more sensational in the flesh. Do you remember how you felt when you first looked into the face of the most famous man on the planet?
The vibes were just like I was standing next to a high-voltage pylon, and that was without him even trying.

You've probably been asked this a thousand times Jim, but the obvious questions usually have the most interesting answers. Tell me what he was really like as a person.
Super, shy, sensitive and spectacular.

I was told some time ago that Elvis made some comments about your hair and a photograph of him inspecting it seems to back that up. What did he really have to say?
"Is it a wig?" he asked.
"No," says I. "Give it a pull."
Hey presto, a super picture!

What did you guys talk about? Was Elvis interested in one particular topic or was it just polite banter between you both?
Well, I actually met him seven or eight times through Colonel Tom Parker and

Tom Diskin. I met him on the set of *Roustabout* and *Wild in the Country* too. It was good general chat, although I made sure not to bore him.

Did the Colonel insist on you wearing the promotional coat for the pictures or did you think it was a bit of fun?
Yes, it was the Colonel's coat, but I just wore it for a bit of fun.

Did you watch any of the filming?
Plenty, it was a mind-blowing experience.

I'm sure most of your colleges at radio Luxembourg were envious to say the least, who was most excited about your meetings with Elvis?
All the listeners really, even today people ask to shake the hand that shook the King's.

And finally Jim, how should we remember Elvis, and how do you remember him personally?
He 100% deserves the unique fan loyalty. He was a star and everyone's brother at the same time.

> **"** Rarely a day that goes by without a little bit of Elvis appearing somewhere in my life. **"**

Tamara Beckwith

Hi Tamara. Thanks for giving us your time. Firstly, I'm interested to know what you thought of the *Finding The Way Home* CD that I recently sent you. Did the language bother you?
I think that the unofficial material you sent me was great. Personally, I'm all for showing the real Elvis and not the sugar-coated version so normally fed to us. As for the swearing, I think most of us would have known he wasn't a saint.

I loved all the outtakes and have listened endlessly.

What about the video footage? Are you the kind of fan that can sit and watch a tape full of 8mm cine film that is far from perfect in picture and sound quality?
The video footage was great and so fabulous to have as something a little special. Most of us were not lucky enough to have met him or even seen him in the flesh so a few stolen moments are something to cherish.

So, how long have you been a fan?
I have been an Elvis groupie since I was pretty small, both my parents are Elvis fans and so we often had his music in our house. I remember when he died we were in Greece and the hotel had a moment of silence before dinner out of respect.

Do your friends think you're crazy?
Most of my friends do not share the same passion for Elvis and in fact, many refuse to drive in my car due to my taste in music in general. A couple of my girlfriends agree that he was utterly gorgeous, but that's where they draw the line. Both my sister and my daughter adore him and his music though.

They don't know what they're missing eh? Whether it's in the car or at home, do you find time to actually listen to Elvis music?
Hand on my heart, there's rarely a day that goes by without a little bit of Elvis appearing somewhere in my life.

Do you think that other celebrities that love Elvis should shout about it a bit more?
I think that everybody is entitled to his or her privacy and most people in the limelight like to keep their private lives just that - private. I'm sure those who genuinely love Elvis would be quite happy to say so. I don't think Elvis could be very much more alive in people's hearts do you?

You're right but it's so good for Elvis when people like yourself and Frank Skinner openly admit to being fans. Did you catch Frank's programme about the shirt by the way?
I did not get to see the programme on Elvis' shirt as I was in LA, but I think it was more out of wanting to create a show for Elvis rather than the shirt alone.

Yes, I think Frank was happy giving fans a positive program about Elvis. It helps to make it all that bit more trendy.
I don't think it will ever be trendy to be

an Elvis fan since he is dead and his prime was so long ago. It's either something you get or not. I think part of his charm is that he appeared to be so wholesome yet had the looks of a bad boy, combined with his mummy-boy reputation and that of being utterly irresistible to almost the entire female race. Quite a complicated man I'd say.

You'd be good as a convention guest Tamara, have you ever been to an Elvis event?
I'm not really one for conventions and even though I'm sure I would find it fascinating, I'm not sure it's for me.

Almost every picture I see of you, whether it's in the papers or in a magazine, you seem to be wearing some kind of Elvis T-shirt. Do you have a wardrobe full by any chance?
Elvis T-shirts are my speciality, especially since I met and befriended a couple that have a label called Elvis, Jesus & Co. Couture, who kindly gave me many. Also Adhoc in London has quite a good selection for those of us who like small T-shirts.

I've got to ask, what's your favourite when it comes to Elvis movies? Do you have a favourite song too?
My favourite film would have to be *Jailhouse Rock* just for that one amazing scene in the jail. As for songs; well, that's a hard one since I have so many but *Suspicious Minds, America, The Beautiful* and *Love Me Tender* would have to be in my top ten.

So, as big Elvis fan, have you ever made the pilgrimage to Memphis?
I have just made a plan to go to Graceland with my sister for my daughter's upcoming birthday, so watch this space...

Fantastic, I'll look forward to a full report. Before we close, how do you think Elvis should be remembered?
I think Elvis should be remembered as a human being first and foremost. He was undoubtedly a talented musician and had the voice of an angel. We should also remember that he had his problems too and that he was far from perfect. If we concentrate on the positive and remember his wonderful showman qualities we will have done him justice.

Great answer. Well, thanks for everything Tamara and have a good time in Memphis.

"Ladies and gentlemen, Elvis has left the building. Thank you and goodnight."

Al Dvorin

Can you start by telling us just when your connection with Elvis began?
I believe you two go back a lot longer than fans think?
Sure. I started working with Colonel Parker in the days of Eddie Arnold and Hank Snow, long before Elvis. I started working with Elvis when they signed him back in 1955. I booked all the acts on the shows with Elvis and then I did the introductions to the shows when Elvis went touring the following year.

Then I took on promotions for the movies like *Blue Hawaii* and *GI Blues* and then the various items used on the tours like pendants, pictures and posters. That's my big connection.

What was Elvis like in the early days?
Well, he wouldn't fly. The first time he went to Hawaii we put him on a boat out of San Francisco and he was so nice. I brought my wife along and he was with his cousin Gene Smith and a couple of his buddies.

He was a beautiful person, talented and very respectful to all the ladies. It was an honour working for the man, really.

What about your famous saying, "Elvis has left the building?"
Did it come about by accident?
It was by accident, yes sir. When he was jumping off the stage I said to Colonel Parker, "What'd I do when he jumps off into the limo?" and he said, "Just tell 'em he's gone Al." So, as he jumped into the car I just said, "Ladies and gentlemen, Elvis has left the building.

Thank you and goodnight." That's how it all started.

It's always fantastic to actually hear you say it.
You know, I hear it all over. I was recently in the Middle East and I hear it coming down the street, they were playing *An Afternoon in the Garden* in a bar. The fans like it and they've now accepted it.

Was it used right back from Elvis' Las Vegas comeback in 1969?
We used it in so many places. I used in during the movie *Elvis On Tour* but I don't think we used it during that particular time, no sir. We didn't use it at the Hilton Hotel in Las Vegas or at the few shows in Hawaii. The Pearl Harbour show and the Memphis charity shows didn't close with it either. It was the stadium shows and on tour when the concerts ended that way. In Memphis we always closed with "Elvis has left for Graceland." Have you heard it?

Yes, of course. It's on the album *Elvis Recorded Live on Stage in Memphis* and you even get a mention on the sleeve notes for it.
Yeah, also on the CD *An Afternoon in the Garden* you can here me saying "Elvis has left the building, thank you and good afternoon." That came out a few years back.

What else did you have to do as an employee?
Well, I had to pitch all the souvenirs, the special Elvis souvenirs. "Get your

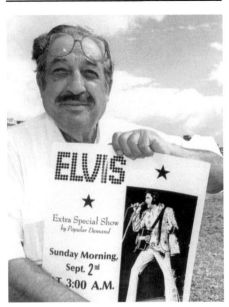

beautiful Elvis picture suitable for framing..." It was ridiculous but they bought the stuff. And also I handled security for the stage but we never talked down to the fans, we only talked to the fans.

When the shows were about to begin I used to say, "You must remain seated because if you approach the stage all you do is block the vision of those seated behind you. They are here to enjoy the show as well as you. Once we commence with the show, please remain seated." It was no problem.

Were you there when Elvis was attacked on stage in Las Vegas in 1973?
Oh yeah, I was at almost all of the shows. I was there when Red and the boys went after the guy. The incident was not that rough so don't believe the stories. Elvis took care of himself and he was a very strong gentleman, but some of his guys got carried away with themselves. Whilst he was on stage that night he let the other guys take care of it. Elvis was just a performer and he

certainly never kicked anyone through a table that night (laughs).

Were the tours as crazy as we've been lead to believe?
No, no not really. It was all very well organised. Elvis had his guys and it was their job to look after him, to dye his hair, to bring him his food and to make sure he got his rest. We had the sound guys, the lighting, we had security, it was a well-oiled organisation right down to the stewardesses for the planes.

Did you travel with Colonel Parker or with Elvis?
Sometimes I travelled with Elvis, sometimes with the Colonel and sometimes on my own. There was no set deal, we'd have our timing down to a fine point and it just worked out well over the years. No problems.

Did everyone get on okay?
There were arguments, but nothing earth shattering.

What was the Colonel really like?
The Colonel was a genius and he and Elvis were good for each other. The Colonel didn't have much formal education but boy, could he twist words around his little finger. When it came to deals, he knew how to make them. He was also very charitable, like Elvis. Between them they gave away so much. I'm telling you, it was fantastic.

He got Elvis top billing, top money, the best conditions, the best dressing rooms and he worked on Elvis day and night. He really didn't have any other interest; Elvis was it. When he was Eddie Arnold's manager he did the same thing for him and the same with Hank Snow too. The Colonel could only work his way and that was for the person he was working for. He was a dear friend to Elvis and a dear friend to me and I'm sorry we lost him.

I never actually had the pleasure of meeting the Colonel but I did receive a

dozen or so cards and letters from him. He commissioned our organisation and he always wished us well. He was very nice to us whilst he was alive.

Yeah, his right hand man, Tom Diskin, was superb too as was all the staff. The present Mrs. Parker was real fine with the fans also. They all did as much as they could for the fans the world over.

Mrs. Parker kindly sent me an order of service from the Colonel's funeral, as we were unable to attend. I was extremely touched, to say the least.

She's a fine lady and a big asset to the Colonel and she's looking after his estate properly.

So what about this equal cut? A lot of fans think it's unfair as Elvis was the entertainer in the partnership.

No, no, let me tell you what I know and won't tell you anything I don't know. It was not a fifty-fifty cut. It may've been true on a concession or something, but from the original contract the Colonel got 25 percent. In later years it changed as the Colonel done a deal with Elvis' father, but in the early days it was just 25. I was there at the start when he signed Elvis, so I know they had a fair deal. Elvis was happy with it, his father was happy with it too. His mother was never happy with anything really. The Colonel kept Elvis under wraps and when he made an appearance it was an event, it was a happening so you've got to give the Colonel a lot of credit. If he'd have signed Elvis with the William Morris Agency they would've over exposed the man. That's really about it.

Going back to Elvis has left the building. It's now so famous, isn't it frustrating that the average person in the street knows it but doesn't know it's you?

Everybody knows the phrase and they know my voice, but the don't know it's Al Dvorin, that's the thing. Sometimes I think Graceland has gone out of its way to keep it a secret. Don't be surprised if you see a big lawsuit.

When you say to people that it's your voice, do they believe you?

No one believes it's me on anything but when they hear my voice they say "Hey, that's really you."

I told a guy in the Middle East that I introduced the Pearl Harbour show in 1961 and he didn't believe me until he bought a book where it states that Al Dvorin produced the show. No, it's my own fault, because when Elvis died I didn't want to do anything. I just sat around and retired. Everyone started taking credit for all the various things that I did and they had fun doing it and they made a lot of money too. Very few people know that I originally created the Elvis Presley Midget Fan Club for instance. What they have in the books is wrong. Joe Esposito's book is wrong too. When Elvis left the stage it was me who made the announcements, never anyone else. Don't believe all you read.

What was it like to have Elvis as a friend?

You couldn't have a better friend. He was good to me, he was good to my wife, he was good to my kids. The first time we went to Hawaii he met my wife for the first time aboard the boat and he treated her like a queen. He had pictures taken with her and everything. He gave her a big kiss and a hug.

What reminds you of him Al?

The memory of his goodness, his religion, his charity, his ability and the very fact that he was one of a kind. There was always a hello, always a smile. He will never be forgotten and the image of Elvis grows every day.

Before we close, can I just thank you for coming over to our shores and putting on such a good show for the British fans?

It was a pleasure and thank you for your hospitality. My wife and I loved it there with you. And listen, I love what you're doing with your magazine and everything. It's so professional and well written. Elvis would've been so proud of you guys.

" Elvis would go right in and perform his number first time and it was perfect. I've never seen anything like it. "

Francine York

Throughout the 1960s, Elvis Presley worked with some of Hollywood's most beautiful women. Many of his movie co-stars were already successful in their careers whilst others popped up and then seemed to disappear never to be seen again. One actress that appeared in a whole series of films before landing a part in *Tickle Me* is Francine York who is still very much in front of the cameras.

Whilst attending high school in Minnesota, Francine won just about every declamation contest she entered and developed a passion for acting by starring as the lead in many school plays.

Her drama coach encouraged the young actress by writing a message in her yearbook, which informed Francine that she would someday carve out a Hollywood career as she certainly had the talent. The Hollywood cameras were still a long way away for 17-year-old Francine but an opportunity did come along in the form of a beauty contest, which was part of the Miss America pageant. Francine entered, became runner-up as Miss Minnesota and the modelling jobs started to roll in.

Moving to Minneapolis, she got a job modelling sweaters for Jane Richard's Sportswear and began travelling all over America, ending up in San Francisco where she took a modelling course to further her skills. Whilst enjoying a fabulous modelling career, Francine won runner-up prize in the Miss San Francisco pageant and then went on to take over the title as the winner became ill.

As one of America's most beautiful women, Francine was in great demand and her movie break came when she met Mary Meade French who took her to Hollywood and to her first agent. After a series of commercials, Francine appeared in her first feature film *Secret File Hollywood*, which premiered in her hometown. The whole town had gathered at the airport to see her arrive and Francine fondly remembers it as being one of the biggest thrills of her life but more was yet to come. Jerry Lewis had seen the film and he was so impressed that he wanted Francine to appear in six of his movies which were to include *It's Only Money*, *The Nutty Professor*, *Family Jewels*, *Disorderly Orderly* and finally *Cracking Up* in 1982 where she plays a noble woman with a French accent from the 15th Century. Francine also went on to star in *Bedtime Story* with Marlon Brando and David Niven, whom she adored.

It was around this time that Francine appeared in many Max Factor adverts shown in the USA and all over Europe and a keen interest in fitness and nutrition bought her to the covers of such national magazines as *Let's Live* and *Fitness Plus*.

Apart from *Tickle Me*, Francine's other film credits include the cult movie *Curse of the Swamp Creature*, *Cannon for Corboda* with George Peppard, *The Greatest Story Ever Told*, *Sergeant Was A Lady* and *School for Bachelors* with Bob Hope and Eva Marie. Francine's impressive list of achievements also include TV appearances such as *The Streets of San Francisco*, *Columbo*, *Kojak*, *Wild Wild West*, *Police Story*, *Mission Impossible* and *Perry Mason*.

After recently guest starring in *Beverly Hills 90210* and *Lois & Clark*, Francine has just completed a movie with Nicholas Cage entitled *Tomorrow Man*. I briefly asked her more about her days with Elvis...

It was great fun watching *Tickle Me* for the first time in a few years and seeing your scenes with Elvis.
Well, there was far more filmed than what you actually see of me. Several close-up scenes where shot but for some reason they were cut from the final film.

How did you get the part?
They were using me in a lot of posters and things at the time so I just went along and auditioned. When I got the part I just couldn't believe I was going to work with Elvis Presley. He was just so fantastic and so handsome. I was already a fan and had been for sometime, ever since watching *Jailhouse Rock*. I was so excited about actually meeting him. He was so gorgeous.

There's a very famous photograph of Elvis teaching you how to shoot an arrow?
You've seen it? The film is set on a health ranch and so there were several scenes in which we were just doing this kind of thing. Norman Taurog came to everybody with a list of activities and it just so happened that I learnt how to use a bow and arrow in high school so I picked it. We filmed a lot more than you actually see and I took a couple of shots at the target. There was something wrong with the lights or the camera angle and so we had to shoot the scene several times. Norman asked Elvis if he'd mind shooting it again, and he said that he wouldn't mind doing it all day. He then pulled me closer and whispered "and all night."

Did you take this as an offer from Elvis?
Well, not really. He was just being friendly I think. It wasn't a good thing to get involved with the people you work with back then. I just took it as a friendly comment.

Was there any activity in the trailers at night?
Oh yeah, Elvis and the guys enjoy themselves with all the beautiful women

What happened to Joyclyn Lane?
You know, I haven't seen her since we finished that movie. She was awful, walking around the set with her nose in the air and her backside sticking out. Everybody disliked her and we'd follow behind her with our noses in the air just making fun of her.

She came across that way in the film too. What did Elvis think of her?
He was very professional, but I don't think he really liked her either. He really was a true professional in the way that he knew his job. Norman would have a stand-in do the songs, just to show Elvis the camera angles and stuff. Elvis would then go right in and perform the number first time and it was perfect. Those songs were fantastic. I've never seen anything like it.

Elvis would mime to those songs and do a pretty good job with no sign of any nerves.
Yes, it was fantastic. I did see him do the sign of the cross when he thought nobody was looking so perhaps he did get a little nervous. But he was so religious with his upbringing and everything.

Was Colonel Parker around?
I didn't see him myself but I think he was there for just one day. I remember everybody talking about it on the set.

And finally Francine, how do you think the world should remember Elvis Presley?
Oh, as the handsome singer with charm. He was so perfect and a real gentleman.

Thanks for your time Francine and what's more, thanks for making the effort to contact us. I know it took you several attempts to reach us but we really appreciate your time.
Its a pleasure. Bye-bye.

in the movie. Elvis had a girlfriend then too and I remember him getting angry when she drove on to the set. He had a few words to say to her and it seemed as though he was upset that she had come to the studio.

Elvis was with Priscilla at the time.
This definitely wasn't Priscilla. I don't remember her name but she had a huge car, a Cadillac or something.

Did you spend any time with Elvis off set?
Yes, we'd sit around and talk between takes. He asked me about modelling and he was very complimentary, especially about my high cheekbones (laughs). It was nice because he always wanted to know about the person he was talking too. You know, it was the first time I'd ever seen a drinks cooler too. Elvis and his guys had all their cokes on ice. We all had a lot of fun.

" I don't really have any restrictions in life but I can imagine what somebody like Elvis went through. It must've been very lonely. "

Harry Hill

Harry Hill is one of the funniest and most successful comedians to ever hit British TV screens. With his own crazy TV show on Channel 4 and several successful nationwide tours, Harry is well and truly on the map when it comes to original and visual comedy.

Harry recently made history when he became the first British comedian to perform stand-up on *Late Night With David Letterman*; the USA's highest rated chat show. It was an unprecedented break through for a comedian with no previous television exposure at the time. David Letterman himself said, "I like that guy - there's something wrong with him" and extended an open invitation to return anytime.

Living in London with his wife Magda and his two young children, we asked Harry to tell us why he's so proud to be an Elvis fan...

Tell us how you first got into Elvis?
Gosh, I don't know really, I've only recently got into him. I remember when he died, I must've been about 12 or something, and I didn't think about it at all then and he didn't mean anything to me at all at that stage because I was a big Beatles fan. My parents were into Frank Sinatra and Shirley Bassey, so I don't think I really heard much of his stuff apart from what was out on the radio, so I never really bought anything back then. I suppose at that time all I really saw was the later stuff, the Vegas sort of blown up image, so I treated it as a bit of a joke because I didn't know much about it. Then much later, my wife and I were a bit curious about the myth, if you like, and we wondered what Graceland was like, so we went along to see where he lived and learn more about him. I realised then that it wasn't what I thought, in other words, I learnt that he was quite a normal man with humble beginnings and that he was kind of exploited. No one else had done what he did and had the success that he had, so what I came away with was just that.

So it was really Memphis itself that kicked it all off for you?
Well yes. Then I read the book *Last Train To Memphis* and I felt that I really started to get to know the man. Until then I'd really only seen him as this kind of Englebert Humperdink type entertainer in Vegas, then after reading the book I really found out what it was all about... the music.

Going back to Graceland, do you feel that the estate has done a good job with things over there?
It's nice for fans to be able to go there, but in a way there's an element that's a bit distasteful because it's exploiting him still, even from beyond the grave. But for me, as a man, it was nice to see the whole thing and to buy some souvenirs.

Is that where you bought your TCB brooch that you often wear on TV?

Yes it was, there's no kind of middle-way with that kind of thing I suppose. I was very surprised by the guards who were obviously Elvis fans and very respectful of him. It wasn't quite the carnival that it could be.

We are lead to believe that the rooms open to the public are the very same areas he would've shown you around if you were lucky enough to be invited up to the house.
From reading my book it was apparent that he was keen on the fans, he'd go down and talk to them and invite them in and stuff. He was very generous in that way and he enjoyed that side of his success.

How did you feel finally standing at his grave? Could you describe you emotions?
Very sad, the whole story is very sad.

Did you write on the wall Harry?
Oh no.

If you had, what would you have written?
Er... I don't know... I once bought this sticker which said 'My Way with Elvis' so I thought that was pretty good. You know, I was very surprised because it's such a small house, a regular kind of place really. Elvis was the biggest entertainer of the age and yet Graceland is smaller than the house George Harrison lived in. It was very humble of him.

The press has always maintained that Graceland was this big prison and he was trapped by his own fame.
That's right, and they also go on about the décor, but I really didn't think it was that over-the-top at all. Elvis died in the 1970s and it's the worst time to die if you're going to leave the house open to the public. I always think that people who got married in the 1970s always have the worst wedding photographs.

I wouldn't want just anybody seeing my old school photo, that's for sure!

Well yes, but it makes them more interesting.

So, if you moved into Graceland tomorrow, you wouldn't be changing much then?
I don't know about that. Perhaps I'd have to modernise the kitchen a bit.

If you don't mind me asking, are your huge collars anything to do with Elvis?
Not directly no, but they are kind of Elvisy aren't they?

Well, they may've given me a small clue as to your liking for Elvis but I really can't remember how I found out that you were a fan.
A mutual friend, Ian Morris I believe, gave me a copy of the CD *Desert Storm*.

I remember supplying Ian with a couple of copies, one for you and the other for Frank Skinner, who played some of the dialogue on his show. Do you recall Elvis as being in serious trouble during that show, especially with that outrageous outburst on stage?
Yes, of course, it was like a sort of cabaret act and he hardly does any songs really. He just races through them and I think that if you went to see him you really wouldn't want him to hang around like that, but no one would really stand up to him and say no. Like that Dr. Nick and that other doctor, Ghanhem or whatever his name was, who constantly prescribed him drugs. Nowadays he would've gone to the Priory or something.

There were no Betty Ford clinics then.
No, and it was also very taboo. If only he had acknowledged it then perhaps someone would've gathered round and forgiven him for it.

I think Elvis could've been a really stubborn man, he thought he always knew best.
Yes, he thought he was in control and he never really admitted that he had a

problem but if the doctors hadn't been so readily available to subscribe them. You know what I mean? If only it was a bit more difficult for him to get hold of them. You need to understand the entire story of how it started and why it started too. Most of the time they were just tranquillisers so it wasn't as if he was getting high, they were to calm him down.

What's your opinion of the guys that were around him? Do you think they were just making the best of a bad situation?
Well, the whole thing snowballed didn't it? I think he had the fellas around him because it was just fun to start with and he'd give them a few gifts and things and he'd then end up relying on them. Friends and money is the worst combination you can get and you should never lend any money to friends.

There have been so many rumours as to how Elvis actually died. As a former doctor, I'd be interested to know your opinion on what happened on that day in 1977.
I think he may've taken too much medication, fell asleep and choked, I'm sure of it. It's been said that he passed out a couple of times whilst he was eating and it's a very risky business.

Elvis obviously had a difficult time with privacy and I wondered if you ever find things difficult when it comes to being recognised? Are you going through the same thing as Elvis did?
Well yes, to a certain extent, but in a tiny way and I do have an idea of how he must've felt. I don't really have any restrictions in life but I can imagine what somebody like Elvis went through. It must've been very lonely, as you can't

didn't actually appreciate good music. He saw it as just entertainment, which it was, but he never had that same passion as Elvis. He saw the audiences reaction and thought of ways to exploit it. During the later years when the Colonel gambled a lot, Elvis never really stood up to him but if he had; who would he have gone with? If he could've got someone who was more sympathetic towards the music the whole thing could've been avoided.

What about the rest of your family Harry? Are your children Elvis fans?
They're still very young, but my wife was into it long before I was. She had a lot of the records and stuff so she kind of got me into it a bit more.

So, do you sit and watch Elvis films together?
I'm not mad keen on the films I'm afraid.

What about the documentaries like *That's The Way It Is* and *Elvis on Tour*?
Yeah, I love all those. There was an Elvis night recently on VH1 and we really enjoyed that.

just go to places where other people go.

Do you think the Colonel did a good job in your opinion?
Well, I think if Elvis had changed his management when things started to go on the slide after he started working the hotels, then it may've injected something new into his life. I think that the Colonel

Have you ever seen the CBS TV special from 1977?
That's the one that was recorded just a few weeks before he died right?

That's it.
No, I haven't. I've seen the clip of Elvis singing *Unchained Melody* at the piano, which was...

His voice was better than ever then.
Absolutely, but he should've been in the clinic instead of on stage.

Elvis harmed his own image towards the end didn't he?
Yes, I think it was harmful to his image. I used to do a stand-up routine which was a bit disrespectful and that was before I really got into him. I think it was a popular view back then with the guy bingeing and stuff. People only know what they're fed, it's what they read in the tabloids and they don't go into in any detail. Older people will remember when he first came out and obviously they don't have that same view.

What do you think of impersonators?
Well they're nothing to do with Elvis are they? I can take them or leave them. The person they make a fool out of most is themselves isn't it? That's what we enjoy about them and laugh about. Did you ever listen to that *Gravelands*?

Never heard of it.
This guy doesn't impersonate Elvis and he doesn't look anything like him although he kind of does his voice. He sings modern songs so you get the idea that if Elvis were alive, maybe this would be the kind of songs he'd be doing. I don't know what the story behind it is but it's actually very interesting.

Did you get to see *Elvis - The Concert* during the recent UK tour?
I was curious about it but then I started thinking that if I'd have gone then maybe I'd have ended up disappointed. Have you seen it then?

Yes, several times. It's a great show.
Maybe I'll try and see when it tours again.

Any comments on BMG, do you think they're doing enough for Elvis?
To be honest, I don't really know. My brother once gave me a big box set from Readers Digest and it's still in an immaculate condition. That was a great collection.

Gone are the days when you used to get sniggered at for being an Elvis fan. It's almost trendy to be a fan nowadays. Maybe this is down to so many top celebrities openly admitting that they are into Elvis?
The same thing happened to John Lennon to a certain extent, when they die there's this huge reaction which is extreme and unbalanced and then as time goes by, it gets forgotten.

Gradually, you get left with a true idea of what it was all about and when the dust settles you get left with the normality. It happens particularly with entertainers but in the end people appreciate what it was about and what that person actually achieved. You'll always end up with just the good stuff. You've got some events coming up?

That's right, we're planning on bringing over more USA guest stars, people who were actually around Elvis and who can tell a first hand story.
I met Elvis' stepbrother once, David Stanley. I was waiting to do an interview on Capital Radio and there was this guy sitting next to me in this cowboy hat. I didn't know who it was at first but after I did my interview they announced that Elvis' stepbrother was next so then I knew who he was. He was a big fella.

Well Harry, thanks for being part of Essential Elvis and thanks for taking the time talk to me about your passion for Elvis, it's been interesting and it's appreciated.
No problem.

"To this day, I have never met anyone with such charisma. He made the room electric, and it was as thick as London fog.**"**

Deborah Walley

Although she was mainly known for her many roles in beach movies, Deborah Walley actually started out on the stage in New York. Her parents were professional figure skaters, which meant that Deborah did a lot of travelling with them during the summer but spent her school months with a nanny in New York. After studying at the Academy of Dramatic Arts, she began getting various roles on Broadway until talent scout Joyce Selznick saw her in Chekhov's Three Sisters. She was then asked to audition for episodes of the TV series *The Naked City* and *Route 66*.

This led to the role of Gidget in *Gidget Goes Hawaiian*, her first film.

A couple of Disney films followed and then it was straight back to the beach for such classic movies as *Beach Blanket Bingo*, *It's A Bikini World*, *The Ghost In The Invisible Bikini*, *Dr Goldfoot* and *The Bikini Machine* and of course *Spinout* with Elvis. In the film, Deborah plays Les, the pseudo-androgynous drummer in Elvis' band who has to repeatedly remind the other musicians that she's a girl due to her boyish looks. Along with Shelley Fabares and Dianne McBain, Deborah's character Les tries to snare the leading man but of course, Elvis tries to remain single in the face of all the attention.

Can you start by telling us how you got the part of Les in *Spinout*?
It was actually written for me, so I didn't have to audition. I had just worked with Norman Taurog, the director, in another film and we got on very well and we were very good friends until he died in the early 1970s.

Elvis and Norman got along very well too didn't they?
Yes, Elvis liked him very much; he was a wonderful director. An original script for Les in *Spinout* didn't exist as there was just a guy drummer in the band and the whole competition over Elvis didn't initially involve me. *Spinout* was one of the favourite films I did because of that part.

Did you have to learn to play the drums?
The producer bought me a drum kit and sent a teacher to my house every day, every afternoon except for Sundays, for eight weeks. I practiced all the time so that I could actually play by the time we shot the film. Obviously, my neighbours weren't too pleased.

Can you still play the drums?
Oh, I don't know. I have a lot of musician friends and I used to sit in when they'd be playing a club. I used to keep a pretty good beat and I probably still could.

Describe your first meeting with Elvis.
I was not an Elvis fan before making the film. I was from New York and my taste in music was a bit more sophisticated. I liked classical music but around that time it was actually the Beatles that got me interested in rock 'n' roll, not Elvis. I didn't think an awful lot of him as an actor, but I was wrong, I will say that. Those scenes where I'm setting up the table and we're putting up the tents, that was choreographed like a dance number and we worked on it for about a week. I wasn't all gaga about working with Elvis Presley, but when he came into that rehearsal room, with a couple

of his boys with him, I was so astounded.

To this day, I have never met anyone with such charisma, it made the room electric, and it was as thick as London fog. I was stunned and as he walked over to me my mouth dropped. He put out his hand, which I took, he looked into my eyes and said "It's such a pleasure to meet you and to be working with you, I am such a fan of yours."

That was an extremely nice thing to say. How did it make you feel?
I was totally wrapped around his little finger. He was very down-to-earth and not at all full of himself. He was very humble in fact; he told me that he should really still be driving a truck.

Do you remember the Colonel being around on the *Spinout* set?
I remember seeing him around a bit but I don't have a high opinion of the Colonel.

What about Elvis' guys?
They were particularly nice to me. I got along great with the West cousins in fact, I still see Red and I used to see Sonny a lot but I haven't seen him in quite some time. Sonny was a good friend but he's moved now, to Nashville I think. I remember Joe Esposito who I still see and I'm in touch with. I'm very fond of Joe; he's great. Oh, there was Richard...

Richard Davis?
Yeah, I remember him very well.

Joe, Red and Sonny actually appear in the film as extras right?
Right.

When did you last see the film?
I can't remember.

Tell me about the stray dog you adopted on the set.
It was actually a German shepherd. We were out on location at a kind of rocky wilderness in LA filming the race scene

" *Elvis was very clear about what he was saying. He said he wasn't going to live a full life, that he was going to exit early.* **"**

and Elvis and I were sitting near a creek under some trees waiting to work. We were deep in conversation when this dog wondered up, real skinny and mangy looking and it seemed very lost. Elvis was so concerned about this dog that he got Sonny and Richard, I think, to go down to the store to get some dog food. We fed the dog then Elvis sent it down to the groomers to get a bath. Joe bought it back and the dog stayed with us for the day. Elvis had the boys go and put up signs and call the animal rescue people to say that it had been found. At the end of the day, what can you do? The dog rode with Elvis and I in his Rolls Royce back to my house and we never heard anything about it so I kept it for many years after that. I called her Missy.

That's a great story. Elvis was very caring wasn't he?
He loved animals and he loved children.

Did Elvis talk about Priscilla much?
Yes, she was around at the time but he didn't talk much about her. One day when I was up at his house he did show me her picture.

Do you remember where Elvis was living at the time?
It was in Bel Air but I really can't remember which house. I remember that it was very modern and I could still probably draw a picture of the room but I can't recall the exact address.

It was probably Perugia Way.
That's it. It was Perugia Way.

When Elvis showed you Priscilla's picture at the house, did he sound like a man in love?
I can't say that he did.

Did he mention the wedding?
Well yes, he said they were going to get married, I remember that.

Our conversations were almost always focused on spiritual matters so he didn't go on about Priscilla that much at all. Elvis had been greatly influenced by Larry Geller who was his hairdresser. Larry was on, and still is on, a spiritual path and so Elvis was really into it back then.

Could you identify with this kind of talk at the time? Was it all a bit strange?
Oh, it was all very new to me. He started off very gently but I had been raised Catholic and my experience with the church was a turn-off and I was not on good terms with God. It was a dark night of the soul, a void of not feeling one way or the other but if you had asked me at the time if I believed in God, I would have probably said that I didn't. I had never heard of the concept of reincarnation or anything Elvis was throwing at me.

So did Elvis finally get you round to a different way of thinking?
He was one of the most influential people that I'd ever met and he really changed my life. I was never the same after Elvis, especially in terms of spirituality and the path that I began with Elvis; I'm still on it today. It grows, it changes and it expands but in a kind of odd way, Elvis was a guru to me and I was a very eager pupil. I think Elvis found in me an empty vessel into which he could pour all the knowledge that he had acquired. We talked about Buddhism, Hinduism and all types of religion. He taught me how to meditate; he took me to the Self-Realisation Centre and introduced me to Yogananda. We talked a lot for a long time.

How long did the filming take?
Several months, it was a full on schedule.

Did you go anywhere else to talk apart from the movie set?
Unfortunately, Elvis couldn't go anywhere so it was either my house or his house. There were no parties, it was just he and I talking, eating ice cream, big bowls full of ice cream.

How long did this friendship last? Did you see him after the film was completed?
I didn't see him a lot, but we kept in touch.

When was the last time you talked?
It was just a couple of years before he passed away. During that time period he seemed to change a bit.

In what way?
Ah, it's hard to put my finger on it.

Would you say he became disinterested in things?
Yeah. But I'll tell you something; he told me that he wasn't going to be around for very long, he was done. He was very clear about what he was saying. He said that he wasn't going to live a full life that he was going to exit early.

Was this something that he thought God had planned for him?
He felt that what he had to do was completed and that he had to go and he wasn't going to be around very much longer. I think that in the last few years he was not happy, he was not happy for quite a while. It was almost as though he was put here and he had to do what he had to do.

You worked with Elvis during the later part of his movie career and it's been well documented that he disliked a lot of his films. How did this affect his state of mind?
I know that he really wanted to get more into acting and he did have a talent but he wasn't allowed to really show it. It was just the kind of material and the way they wrote for him.

Beach movies were very fashionable at the time weren't they?
I really identified with him regarding the films because my career was going the same way. I started on Broadway and my whole dream was to be an actress on the stage and because of my mother and other people who were able to control my life, I was terribly young when I started, my career got caught up in what Hollywood wanted. It took away what my dream was, what I wanted. Elvis and I talked about that because we both related to it. He liked the kind of movies he did like *King Creole* with a little bit more meat to them. He wanted to do a James Dean role but the Colonel forbade it.

What about the way things ended up?
I don't think anybody really knows the truth about what happened and I don't know either. I wasn't there when it happened but the last time I talked to him he told me about the pain he was in and that he was having a lot of health problems. So he took a lot of those prescription drugs just to kill the pain but once you start taking them, you have to start taking more because they just don't work anymore.

In finishing, how should the world remember Elvis Presley?
Not only as someone who totally gave a birth to a new music but also as someone who changed the entire music industry. Also, as probably the most impactful entertainer we've ever known. But more than any of that, the goodness that he set in motion. His fans are the greatest fans ever and each fan club has charities, a lot of them for children. They all work very hard in raising money for various good causes. In a way, Elvis was like a pebble thrown into a still pond and all the ripples have gone out all over the world. He lives on. His spirit lives on.

" I love working with Elvis footage...

Believe me, I will get you guys

everything I can. "

Rick Schmidlin

Rick Schmidlin is a man whose feet are being kissed by Elvis fans from all over the world. He recently produced the special theatrical edition of *Elvis: That's The Way It Is* for Turner Entertainment and Turner Classic Movies. The film was completely re-cut and re-mixed and included in this new version are nine additional new musical performances and many never-before-seen personal moments of Elvis working with his band.

It premièred before 2,500 screaming fans in Memphis 2000 at the Orpheum Theatre as the main theme of Elvis Week 2000 and Rick was there to say a few words prior to the showing.

Rick has been an Elvis fan since he saw *Roustabout* in 1964 when it was first released in a theatre in Hackensack, New Jersey. Of the thousands of records and CDs in his collection, Elvis out numbers them all by ten to one.

During 1979 through to 1980, Rick was the assistant light director at The Whiskey au Go Go on Sunset Boulevard in West Hollywood. Later, as a lighting director, he toured the US and Europe with various bands before going on to produce music videos.

Now, Rick is the only filmmaker to ever receive awards two consecutive years in a row from The National Society of Film Critics and The Los Angeles Film Critics Association. What is also remarkable is that these were special awards and not in a specific category.

Andrew Hearn talked to Rick at the world premier of *Elvis: That's The Way It Is* in Memphis, where he was more than happy to answer several questions.

What is your title and job description for the newly edited *TTWII* movie?
I worked as produced and oversaw all creative aspects of the production.

What did your job involve?
I supervised all research, selected my team, and had a hands-on involvement from the very first day. This for me was a seven a week 18-20 hour a day job. There was not one aspect of the process that I wasn't totally involved in. I'm a real hands-on kind of filmmaker.

What are your views on the final result? Are you proud of the film?
The first time I really saw the completed film in all its glory was with you and the many fans in Memphis and it gave me chills. I was completely delighted that I was able to do this project, it is the most exciting thing I've ever done and the highlight of my career as filmmaker.

Who was responsible for discovering the new footage?
It was a team effort, no one person can be singled out. Just when you thought you had it all somebody on my team or myself would find more. Some of this material was two miles underground in a vault in Kansas, other material was five minutes from the editing room. I am a research hound and never satisfied that I've found everything, this causes many sleepless nights.

What's the truth on the possible cinema release in the UK?

The talk is good and there is serious talk too. I will do my best to see that it plays in ever location in the UK that will have it. I know it would be very successful.

Is the DVD/video release of January 2001 a worldwide release?

That I don't know yet.

All Elvis DVDs to date are poor quality in comparison to other releases. Will the newly edited version of *TTWII* be of a higher standard?

Yes, from what I am told this will be first-rate job and that Warner Home Video will spare no expense.

Any news on the extra footage being added to the DVD and will this be added to the video too?

I have wonderful material to work with and right now we are seeing what we can fit in.

I am a fan as well as a filmmaker and don't want anyone to feel cheated, including myself.

Will there be a 'making of the movie' on DVD as rumoured?

Yes, Turner Classic Movies has made one. Tom Brown who works there is a huge Elvis fan and is from Tupelo. This project is for him as important as it is for me and you, so expect a first rate job from someone who really loves Elvis.

Can you give any news on the interactive part of the DVD?

Not at this time, but we may try to put a multiple angle selection on a song to let the viewer control the shots. I will need to pick the song that has the most coverage.

It's been speculated that if the DVD/video release does well, there'll be an out-take video release in the Autumn of 2001, any truth in this?

I haven't heard that one.

As MGM/Warner Brothers is cataloguing all the material they have from *TTWII* and *Elvis On Tour*, is there a possibility of a collector's video package? Something along the lines of BMG's *Follow That Dream* collector's CDs but on DVD would be fantastic.

That again is up to the gods at Warner Home Video. I am just the lonely filmmaker, but if they want to do anything I am committed to stay on board and help in anyway I can. It is really Turner Entertainment and Turner Classic Movies that is behind this. MGM has no involvement at all. Roger Mayer, president of Turner Entertainment, is the man who championed this project and made it possible. Elvis fans around the world have a lot to thank this man for - he is our saviour.

What about producing some hour-long specials for TV only?

Everybody thinks there is really a lot more then there is. I would say that at best I have found enough unseen footage to fill up to sixty minutes in time. They did not shoot every song. Certain people think that everybody has held back material and that is not the case.

Single camera performances will have to be used to make that sixty minutes happen. It was very hard to make the cut of the film we had. My goal was to give the fan everything that we can find that works. I personally am not holding back anything, that statement has been made by those who have not spent the time I have with this material. So, please understand that there is not and never was enough footage for even three hours with what we have. This film was shot with film not video like CBS special. It is hard to be accused (not by you) by those who think they know more then you after spending a year of sleepless nights just hoping to find more.

Are there plans for an updated edition of *Elvis on Tour* and will you be involved in the project?

There is talk, but nothing else yet. Talk is good that's how the filmmakers seeds get planted, it's how it all starts.

I am in this for the long haul and if it happens I am totally committed to Elvis and his worldwide fans.

I've heard MGM filmed an entire show with Elvis wearing the Fringe jumpsuit?

MGM never shot an entire night. In fact, the opening fringe suit is all we have. There are stills, but the footage was not shot. Today on video we shoot everything but then it was pick and choose and they had never shot a concert like this before on film. I have read that myth about three to four hours and it just does not exist.

How easy was it to omit certain songs like *I've Lost You*? Also, why was *I Just Can't Help Believin'* left out, especially as Elvis makes several references to forgetting the words pre-show. It's probably one of the most well known Elvis tracks too.

The reason the footage was taken out was because if you look at the original the cutting style was different and we knew fans already had this material. Remember, in 1970, editors did not cut much concert footage. Now our editors have twenty years experience. If those songs would have been included it would have been jarring compared to the new cut and we thrived to major a fluid show. Also, we wanted as much material as we could that featured everybody on stage. It was hard to cut *I Just Can't Help Believin'* but it is not lost, we have the original release too.

I've got to ask; are you sure there's not enough footage for another release?

Remember that I am an independent producer and not a studio employee. I have had access to all files and the vaults, if I could find more I would. I love working with Elvis footage but reality is reality. So believe me, I will get you guys everything I can and I am not out to continue to milk you with new found footage for the next three or four years unless it is new found footage and then we will all win.

Thanks for your time Rick and thanks for a fantastic movie too.

It was awesome. No problem.

" Elvis told us that he was in control,
he knew what he was doing
and he could stop whenever
he wanted to. "

Sonny West

As long as I can remember, the name Sonny West has been lodged up there in my brain filed right alongside Elvis Presley. When I was a kid I can remember being a little scared of Sonny, I thought that he had a pretty evil look about him with those piercing eyes and tough image. For some reason I had the impression that if I ever met Sonny, he'd kill me. Maybe he'd just pick me up and throw me against the wall or he might just draw out that Magnum and tell me to beat it. When I was growing up, Sonny West was the guy I wanted as a big brother, as a guy that would come down to the school and scare the other kids in the playground half to death. I think it was the press conference with Dave Hebler [seen in *This is Elvis*] that painted the picture of this cool, hairy dude that was always pretty angry.

Well, last summer I met Sonny, he didn't kill me and he wasn't angry. I've never been so wrong about a person in my life in fact, the hard-nut Sonny West I expected turn out to be quite soft spoken, ultra-polite and very friendly. Now a born again Christian, Sonny is still very devoted to his beautiful wife Judy (who he married in 1970, with Elvis as best man) and a content family man. He lives a clean life drinking diet Dr. Pepper and talking openly about those wild days with Elvis.

Sonny and I are now close friends talking often on the phone and, as big John Wilkinson recently told me, his only crime was that he loved Elvis too much. We sat and talked in great detail during my last trip to Memphis in August 2000 and I'm honoured and thrilled to print that very interview.

Could we start by you telling us a little about how you first came to meet Elvis?
I first met Elvis in 1958 at the Rainbow skating rink in Memphis, Tennessee but I had seen him before that when he came over to my high school. I was in the tenth or eleventh grade and he came over the campus there and sang a few of his songs. *That's All Right* and some of those others songs the he had out on Sun records. They'd already been cut, the records were out and he was down there promoting them. When I saw him I thought 'man, this guy's talented' but that was the last time I saw him until '57 or '58 at the Tucson rodeo grounds. He did a concert there and I went to see him.

What were you doing for a job then?
I was in the Air force there at Tucson, and then I got out and found another job and met Elvis again in '58 like I said. I had quite an experience there with this girl named Melinda who was a very good skater. She kept knocking me

off because I couldn't skate very well and Elvis noticed it. I didn't know until later but he told me he was watching and that he saw how I took it. I didn't get mad at the girl or anything, I just crawled over the to side and rested. So, he said to Red, "Look, I really like your cousin".

Who arranged the meeting at the rink?
Red did. He bought in my three sisters my brother-in-law and myself. We were introduced to him but he knew two of my sisters already. In fact, Elvis had a big crush on Caroline when she was at Humes High School. She was a cheerleader and a beauty queen and all that. Elvis told me that he had the biggest crush on her but he never could bring himself to go up and ask her out. So, we met him then, and in 1960 I saw him again, when he got out of the army. We worked out at karate a little bit and then he asked if I would go to work for him. I gave notice at my job and went out to California with him on the train.

Did you feel nervous about working for Elvis Presley?
No, it was very relaxed.

What were your initial duties?
A lot of it was just working out at karate. Red and I had grown up on the streets and we could handle ourselves. I had good balance and everything and he liked that. I would help with the cars or anything that he needed. If he needed anything from the store I'd jump in the car and get it, whatever he needed. The security wasn't such a big thing when he was making the pictures because there were security guards at the studio and on the gate and you just couldn't get in there.

When did Elvis feel the need for bodyguards?
The real heavy security started when he started back touring again and that wasn't because of bad people but people unintentionally hurting him.

There were a few nasty incidences involving death threats and things?

Yeah, I think the first one happened in 1971 up there in Las Vegas, which was over the Nevada state line, which is why the FBI came in. It was very serious and they were very aware that it really could happen. There are nuts up there quite capable of killing people. It got real heavy back then but up until that time it was really taking care of the odd guy that wanted to take a swing at him. But after that Manson thing happened we got serious and we carried weapons.

I got a legal right to carry a firearm, I got a permit to carry a gun in Las Vegas, here in Memphis and I carried one in California too. The only place I didn't carry a gun was up in New York because nobody carried a weapon there except policemen.

> **" We were offered money not to write Elvis: What Happened? So we could've walked away."**

Even the Mayor in Los Angeles had a LAPD bodyguard with him. I forget his last name. He was very quiet, very unassuming but very capable. He went up to New York with the Mayor and was told to hand over his weapon. He refused and they told him that if he didn't, he wouldn't be able to enter the State.

Was Elvis told about the death threats?

Well, he had to be told about them so he could be aware at those times but he really knew all about that first one in Las Vegas. He pulled Red, Jerry (Schilling) and myself aside and told us that if anything happened, we had to get at him before the police got him. He wanted us to mess him up real bad.

Did Elvis have any input as to how his own security was arranged?

We had a thing one time in 1975 when we did that New Years Eve show at the Pontiac Silverdome. There was a retarded-type guy in town that was always making death threats against people and the local police came to me and told me about it. They said he'd never acted on any of his threats but I told them that I'd feel a lot better if they could possibly take him into custody. Elvis was going to fly in, do the show and then fly straight out again so I asked if they could hold him for four or five hours and they agreed. They arrested him an hour before Elvis arrived and they kept him there until we were back on the plane.

I didn't tell Red, I didn't tell Elvis, I didn't tell anyone about it because it was handled. Well, a day or two later we were up at the house, the guys and everyone, and there was a policeman there who had a friend at the sheriff's department in Pontiac. He said to Red that he'd heard about the death threat Michigan and so Red asked me about it. I told him that it was handled and the guy was in police custody during the show, the guy was always doing it and I just didn't want to take any chances. Elvis then said to me, "Sonny, why the hell didn't you tell me about that death threat?" and I had to explain it all again. Elvis insisted that I still should've informed him about the guy.

I thought that I didn't really need to tell him because there he was up there on a stage fifteen to twenty feet high, the highest stage he's ever been on, and he was very vulnerable. The band was on another level and the orchestra was on the bottom stage so he was really up there all by himself. I told Elvis that I was concerned about him that night and that it wasn't like Vegas were there were bodies all around and we were close to him. We couldn't have got to him quickly that night if we needed to so I agreed to tell him everything after that.

Red and I talked about it and I told him what Elvis had said. Red said, "I know I heard him. Sonny, if something like that comes along and you've got it handled, just tell me and it'll never go this far again. If Elvis says anything tell him that we've talked about, we had it under control and we didn't want to worry him." Red told me that he would back me up if it ever happened again but it didn't because the next year Red and I were both fired.

There's been a lot of speculation surrounding your departure from the group. What really happened?

Well, we were trying to get him off of his prescription medicine and we were threatening some of the other guys around him. Some of the acts, the vocal groups, were getting stuff to him that they were getting from doctors. We told them to stop it or we were going to hurt them and turn the doctors in to the AMA informing them that Elvis wasn't even a patient of theirs, but medicine is getting to him. These guys were getting medication in their names and then passing it on to Elvis.

Was Elvis putting them up to that?

Yes, he'd buy them cars and stuff to keep it going.

So it ended up getting nasty right?

We went in to speak to this one guy and Red went through the door and the guy was hiding behind it and he broke his toe. The bottom of the door went over his toe and he was in a lot of pain but Red told him that if he needed to come back another time he was going to break more than just his toe, you know? Well, it just dried up and Elvis noticed that it did. One of the other guys finally told him why he wasn't getting the pills, he told him about us. He called a meeting with us and he had us come in so he could tell us that he knew exactly what was going on and that he wanted us to stop it. He told us that he was in control and that he knew

what he was doing and that he could stop whenever he wanted to.

Sounds like a person that's in deep.

Exactly, he was a person that was in denial that needed no help. Elvis told us to back off and Red said, "Well, what about the good old days when you didn't need it?" and Elvis replied, "There are no more good old days." Right then I knew we were on a downward spin you know? Elvis then said, "If you don't back off you're going to be looking for other jobs." So we didn't hold back, we started to do more little things like emptying out drug capsules when they came in we re-filled them with aspirin and stuff. Six months later we were fired because we refused to stop.

How did Elvis fire you after almost twenty years?

He told his father to give us just enough money to live on for two or three months because eventually he was going to hire us back but he had to show us he was still the boss. Linda Thompson was there and she gave the figure of $5,000.00, but instead of doing that, Vernon gave us three days notice, one week's pay and told us he was cutting back on expenses. That wasn't it at all. Elvis was getting pressure from different people in the organisation saying that we were really going to mess things up and I think that he had to have his stuff, he didn't want us and so we left. We were very hurt and so we talked about it and decided that the only way to get things done was to give him a challenge.

So the challenge came in the form of a tell-all book?

We decided to write a book telling how he was hooked on prescription medication and that he needed to get off them. Since then people like Jerry Lee and Dean Martin come out and say they were all hooked. So we put the feelers out for the book, got positive results and started signing contacts. Now this is what a lot of people don't know, we were offered money not to do the book so we could've just walked away. We were told to name a price by John O'Grady, Elvis' private detective who worked for twenty-six years investigating the use of Narcotics in LA. He called us at a hotel called The Continental on Sunset Boulevard; we were with Steve Dunlevey (from America's Star Magazine) in his suite doing the interviews for the book. Steve told me there was a call and I thought it was from my wife or something but it was John. I took the call on the extension in the bedroom and after we said hello John explained, "I'm calling about a certain party that I represent. I won't name any names, but I just want to tell you that I've been authorised by this particular person to ask you guys to come up with a figure for not doing the book." I replied, "Come up with a figure? That's not what it's all about John. We've signed contacts and we've already got advances."

John O'Grady told me that I wasn't hearing him right saying that if we just got up and walked away we'd not need to worry about any law suits, any money or anything. He just wanted us to come up with a figure. I explained that there were three of us doing the book and that we had a good reason for it. I had to talk with Red and Dave and he agreed to call back in fifteen minutes.

I called Red and Dave into the bedroom and I told them that the call was from John O'Grady and that he wanted us to come up with a figure in turn for us not doing the book. They both looked at me and Red said, "You're kidding? Man, we know where that's coming from." I said that I knew what my vote is and the other guys agreed.

This really blows the belief that you guys did the book for money doesn't it?
Exactly, we could've made easy money right there. If we let him off then he would have always known that he could buy his way out of anything. We could have probably got a quarter of a million a piece, or maybe half a million, for

giving up the book that day. We never even discussed a figure or even talked about the offer after that.

Would you say that the book came out far too late to make a difference?
It did and if only you knew the amount of people that have come up to me saying, "God, if only you'd written that book a year earlier." and people have thanked us saying that we had Elvis as long as we did because of you. A lot of fans got irate and mad about it back then but they've read it again and it's been many, many years since someone has said that they don't like our book. So many more actually approach me to say that they understand why we did it.

It's a very tame book compared to what's been written since. The Goldman book for instance.
That's another story there with that Goldman book. I mean, I was told when I was being interviewed for it that it was a really good and in-depth study of Elvis but I wasn't into all that. I just knew that he was killing himself and that he was hurting the people around him, the people that loved him. Albert Goldman came to my house and interviewed me twice for three or four hours at a time. But I told him that if he asks me about something that I don't want to talk about then I wouldn't. I warned him that I didn't want to be misquoted and I didn't want anything taken out of context. He said that if he prints what I say it would be my exact answer and that was fair enough. He even sent me an autographed book when it was finished but I didn't read it, I just put it away. Then I started hearing things and I said, "Now wait a minute." I went to that index page and found my name and I looked up those pages and sure enough, there isn't a single misquote or derogatory comment about Elvis that came from me.

Anyway, I got Albert's number from Lamar and I called him and said, "Albert, I want to tell you something. I

have to say that you were fair to me about not taking what I said out of context, but I think you wrote one of the most horrible books about one of the most wonderful human beings in this world. I don't ever wish to see you or talk to you again."

Do you think Lamar made the wrong move in agreeing to be part of the Goldman book?

I think Lamar was pulled into it. Lamar initially thought Goldman was going to do a really good book.

Tell me about your famous press conference, seen in the movie *This is Elvis*.

On *Good Morning America* the morning after Elvis' death, Geraldo Rivera and Steve Dunlevey were talking on the programme with Steve Hartman. I'm sitting there watching it and these two guys are talking about Elvis as if they knew him, but Dunlevey only knew what we'd told him. Geraldo Rivera based his story on the fact that he'd met Elvis two or three times. The guys are arguing on air and I'm getting so upset with these people bickering back and forth and so I called our attorney to organise a press conference for that afternoon. Red was away on location at the time so I called Dave and he met me to do the conference where I had all that hair on *This is Elvis*. That's where Dave said, "How do you protect a man from himself?" which was a classic statement boy. That said it all. I called that news conference and said some things about Dunlevey and Rivera because they had talked about some kind of flirtation with drugs and they'd said we called him a junkie. That word is not mentioned once in our book and that upset me.

I put the record straight and I said that it should have been us there on *Good Morning America* instead. As a result, World News cancelled the tour we were about to do to promote the book. It was over two years later when I started to really promote the book.

Do you still talk with Dave Hebler?

Oh yeah, he's still doing seminars on karate and everything. We did some shows together in May last year.

Dave can handle himself can't he?

You bet. He's a seventh degree black belt and I kidded him during the show saying that I'd get him to go on stage and tell everyone what Elvis used to get him to do. We'd be out on the floor talking to the local policeman and sometimes Elvis would come out and visit with them. Elvis used to have me do my fast draw and no one ever could beat me. Cops kept going up against me, private detectives, regular cops, and I'd have my gun out pointing at them before they even had theirs cleared.

By the same token, Dave had this thirteen-strike move that he did (also seen in *This is Elvis*) so in Carson City I said, "Dave, we need to tell them about those thirteen moves, those strikes that you do in a second and a half on someone." And he said, "Sonny, we need to cut that down to about six or seven." but he's still very fast. Dave had a lot to do with Elvis' interest in karate back then. Elvis saw Dave in Vale, Colorado on his forty-first birthday in January 1976 just after we'd returned from that thing in Pontiac that I told you about earlier. Elvis had files, what they call wrap sheets, on these guys from Mexico and Los Angeles who tried to get on stage in Vegas and got kicked off. He wanted all of them 'done in' man! He wanted those guys killed.

Was this the drugs talking?

Of course, that's what I mean. He said and did things that just wouldn't have happened if he hadn't been under the influence of some sort of medication and it just broke my heart. I used to go on ahead with Colonel Parker to set up security and I'd meet him at the hotel, we'd go up the elevator to the suite. We always had at least half the floor or sometimes the whole floor. If there were about thirty rooms to a floor, we'd take at least eighteen or nineteen of them. It was in College Park, Maryland when the limousine pulled up and I reached in to pull Elvis out. He got out and his hair was all messed up, his eyes were glazed and he was all thick-tongued.

"Hey Sonny how you doin' man?" he slurred. I had never seen him that bad I mean, his hair always looked good and everything but he was in real bad shape. I usually introduced him to all the cops that were going to help us with security by their names individually but that day I just said, "These are the guys looking after us." And he just said a quick hello and we quickly got him inside.

I went back out and immediately called Red and four or five of the other guys, I think Grob and Schilling were there, and I called a meeting. I wanted to know what had happened as Elvis just wasn't right. I told the guys they we need to say a prayer, as he just did not look good. We circled and I asked the Lord to look after him that day and I'll never forget that.

Did he ever try and cover up the mess he got into?
For a long time he never let it affect his performance but towards the end it started to. He'd say, "Oh, I just got up, I'm a little groggy" but that wasn't Elvis. He had such a great sense of humour. There wasn't anyone funnier than him when he was right.

When was the last time you went up to Graceland?
I went in the house for the first time in 1983. I called Jack Soden and asked if I could take a couple of friends up to Graceland, no special tour or anything, and he said it was fine. I went up there and it was kind of rough on me. I went through the front door and looked at the dining room. I stood and thought about the amount of times I'd walked through there. I was able to hang on emotionally because there were people around, but I

didn't go back up there again until two years ago. I was doing some stuff across the street and I saw the line building for the tour and I said to some friends of mine, "Come on guys, I'm gonna try to go up there" and so they got with me. We got up there with the crowds and got in line with everyone else and I walked across the front of the house and I got to where it was two or three people deep. I wasn't looking where I was going but all of a sudden I turned and all I could see was Elvis' grave. I looked at it for a second and got goose bumps. I turned to the guys and said, "I gotta get out of here," and I left.

As I was leaving a lady came up and asked if I was Sonny West. I told her that I was and she said, "I want to thank you so much because I really feel that we had him as long as we did because of you and Red." That touched me boy, and I got a little teary eyed.

What's the strangest thing a fan has ever approached you about?
Well that same woman introduced me to a young man from Mexico, maybe twenty, twenty-one years old, he didn't speak English real well. He asked me why Elvis didn't like Mexican people because he'd heard that Elvis said such bad things. I told him it was all lies and that Elvis loved Mexicans. This guy told me that Elvis was supposed to have said they were greasy haired people. I told him to remember that Elvis was the one who put stuff in his hair to make it greasy and he even dyed it black too. There were many reports about things Elvis was supposed to have said that he never did in fact, he was upset that he wasn't allowed to go into Mexico because of riots.

On the set of *Fun in Acapulco*, Elvis got upset with the director because he got onto a couple of the actors because they spoke broken English. He yelled, "Jesus Christ, can't you get the lines right?" Elvis took him aside and said, "Sir, those people were hired by the producer, he knew how they spoke and he knew their language, but he wanted them and they're doing the best they can. Rehearse with them more or whatever but please don't be doing that. I don't like you doing that to them" and he stopped it.

He did the same with the director of *Easy Come, Easy Go*. Elvis and Pat Harrington got along really great and they were doing an interior scene on a boat and something had happened, a joke or something, and we were all dying laughing about it. We did about three or four takes and we all kept cracking up each time and all of a sudden the director said, "Okay, that's it. All you guys get off the set" and Elvis said, "Can I see you a minute sir?" He took him aside and told him, "I do these pictures because I have fun doing them. Part of that fun is being with my guys and my friends just having a nice time. If that goes then I go and I won't work on the picture."

The director apologised and said that he didn't mean to upset Elvis to which he replied, "I'm not upset, it's just that my guys are my guys." Elvis went back and talked to Pat for a minute and they did the scene in just one take.

Any tales from other movies?
This same director offered me a bit part, just a line or two, where I have a fight with Elvis in *Roustabout*. Firstly, I was apparently too much of an Elvis type and the director wanted more of a contrast for the fight scene so they gave it to this other guy called Glen Wilder who was a former football player training to be a movie stuntman. If you see *Roustabout,* he's with the real rich guy Toby who throws a punch and Elvis kicks him in the stomach. Guess what this guy does? I've done that shot with Elvis many times and you just drop flat because when he gets you you're out. You don't go into a flip but this guy decides to do just that and Elvis didn't know it. As he went over his heel caught Elvis just by his eye and they had to write it into the script that he had a

motorcycle smash and cut his eye.

Anyway, you can hear the pop on the soundtrack where his heel hits him, pow! Elvis just turns and looks at him with blood flowing down his head and he was just going to go right on with the scene. The guy who hit him was supposed to say something to Elvis but he couldn't get his line out and so the scene was cut. He said, "The way Elvis was looking at me I was ready to get the hell outta there." He knew Elvis wasn't pleased.

Did Elvis have any choice regarding who he worked with, whether it be co-stars or directors?
No, Elvis never picked his director that was up to people like Hal Wallis. It was the same with the leading ladies, they just knew who would work well with Elvis. There were one or two ladies; I don't really want to name names, which weren't what you'd really call beautiful actresses. Elvis didn't have an affair with all of his female co-stars either. Like him and Shelley Fabares never dated, she married Lou Adler, the record producer. Those two made three or four pictures together and they had a good chemistry like Fred Astaire and Ginger Rogers. They had a lot of fun together and she was another of our favourites. She was a very sweet person.

At this point Sonny and I both realised that we only had a few minutes to get down town to the Orpheum Theatre for the world premier of *That's The Way It Is*. We made a run for it, Sonny in his car and me with Marty Lacker. We made it on time and of course, enjoyed the movie.

" When *Patch It Up* was on
I just couldn't stay still.
I had to get up and do that
little move there. **"**

Lionel Hudson

With the exception of one or two reviews, not many Elvis magazines have marked the re-release of *Elvis: That's The Way It Is* with anything really special. This made us come up with the idea to try and trace some of the faces that appeared in the first making of the film in 1970.

Fans throughout the world have wondered about the other people that appeared in the original movie. What ever happened to the annoying goofy guy in the coke bottle glasses? The one who was going to write a dirty little letter? Are the people who married in Vegas still together? What about Sue and Cricket and the cat that liked Elvis music as long as it had a little action in it? All these folks have been left on the cutting room floor second time around except one.

Remember the guy who's standing in front of the RCA boxes asking "What makes me a bona fide fan of Elvis?" before going on to explain why Elvis wasn't doing so good in the early days. Well, Lionel Hudson, is now almost eighty years old. He worked for RCA for sixteen years and also knew Elvis and the Colonel personally. We managed to track down and talk to Lionel about his recollections of the movie and we even got to watch a screening of the original documentary with him too.

By the way, Lionel is the only member of the old gang to still appear in the new edition; as the crazy dancer in the silk scarf giving it some serious dancing during *Patch It Up...* remember?

Tell me where your connection with Elvis and *That's The Way It Is* begins.
I started off as a helper for RCA and we were doing so many records of this gentleman. I had heard of him and knew what he was about but I just couldn't believe that the man could put out that many records. That's when I began listening to him, when I used to go into the sound booths and I started to fall in love with him. Well, whilst I was working at RCA I met a girl who was his fan club president on the West Coast. Her name was Linda and she's in the original movie singing in the choir. She was a very good friend of mine and it was her that recommended me to Mr. Saunders to be in the picture. So, I got in the picture and then to Las Vegas and this is where I really got to meet Elvis.
I could go over to the studio any time I wanted because I was the employee who would transport the tapes over to the producer. At the time I was the only person there working for RCA as a foreman and so this is how I became friends with Elvis and Colonel Parker.

How was Colonel Parker back then?
Oh, the Colonel always took care of me but I was always moving around carrying boxes and stuff. You saw the movie where all the Elvis banners are?

I used to go up there all the time. By this time I had become a foreman and so next time I was in the presence of Elvis was in the studio but he was so busy all the time. Once in a while I'd talk with him and he was a very nice person.

What made Elvis so special to you as an employee of RCA?

The thing that made him special to me is that he was from Mississippi and my father was a very well known doctor there. My mother lived in Jacksonville, Tennessee and they were seventy-five miles apart but when we sat down as a family all we really talked about was Elvis. From then on he's been a part of my life and he's the reason I'm in the business I'm in today.

What kind of things did Elvis talk to you about when you saw him?

Well, Elvis told me that he felt like he was in prison sometimes and although he had everything to be happy about, he was really an unhappy man. I said to him, "Why? You've got everything" and he replied, "You can have all the money in the world but you don't have peace of mind."

Do you think Elvis was envious of the normal man on the street?

He gave some money to me one time and told me to just go and enjoy myself. I thanked him, took the money downstairs in the hotel and I played. I won $22,000.00 because I just didn't care, I just put all the odds on the table and won it all within two hours. I started to get to know him and he talked to me about so many interesting things, especially about the black way of life. He said that things have been written in books about what he'd said about black people and their music. He said that they only printed what they wanted to and not the full story. He said he don't talk about things any more because the more you do, the more they stir it up and use it as a selling point.

How many shows did you see in Las Vegas?

I saw about four or five shows. They were very good as far as I'm concerned but I've looked at so many of them, if you ask me I can't really remember them apart from the show that I was in because everywhere I go people remind me of it. I enjoyed *Jailhouse Rock* and of course, *Patch It Up*.

Fans all over the world will remember you as the guy really losing it during that number.

I tell you, I had no idea that it was going to be that good and I was sitting right down front along with my girlfriend and the music got good with a decent beat. *Polk Salad Annie* was another one and I really wanted to get up on that but when *Patch It Up* was on I just couldn't stay still; I had to get up and do that little move there. It was really something and I really didn't know they were going to be shooting me.

So when you first saw the movie you were totally surprised when you were up there dancing?

Mr. Saunders had a preview at the MGM studios, so I saw it before it got out on the market. I went there and enjoyed the movie but a lot of it they had cut out but I was very well pleased with it.

What was it like watching the original movie again last night?

Let me tell you, last night I felt like I was going back to RCA with all the people who were in the movie. The lady and her mother were my co-workers and as I said earlier, the lady who said he was like a brother was his fan club president out there, so it made me think of those people and that time. Being in that movie has opened so many doors for me, it really has. I can only say that from the time I walked into RCA Elvis has been paying me my wages because he produced so many great movies and records.

" You can have all the money in the world but you don't have peace of mind. "

Do people still recognise you?
I can go virtually anywhere in the United States and someone will recognise me from that movie. I had walked into a place in California and I noticed people just staring at me. After a while one of the waitresses came over and said, "Haven't I seen you some place before?" I said, "I don't think so" and she replied, "Wasn't you in that movie with Elvis Presley?"

What do you think about the loyalty of Elvis' fans?
Do you know something? Elvis still lives on in a lot of people's minds today and some of them didn't really know Elvis but they knew about him. Just like that waitress, they were watching him in the movies and things and by the way, by the time I left that place I had signed four or five autographs.

Are you looking forward to seeing the premier of the new version tonight?
I want to see what they've taken out and what they've put in, but I'm hoping they don't cut me out! But not only that, I'm going to be watching the whole thing all way through.

Have you been up to Graceland?
I've passed there several times but I've only been up there once and it gave me a feeling of happiness and sadness and I just don't like to feel that way. My father used to call me a soft-heart because I would look at things and start crying. I never could understand why I was crying when I should be happy. So, I really don't like to be at the house too much.

Are you having a good time here in Memphis during Elvis Week?
Oh yes, I'm really having a good time because all the people that I meet all really enjoy Elvis and they speak so well of him. We all make mistakes and we all have bad times in our lives but when you're as big as Elvis is in this city, and all over the world, it doesn't matter. He was very good to me and I'm living a very comfortable life because of Elvis. I owe it all to Elvis.

Elvis really is fondly remembered isn't he?
He was a person that was loving and kind. He was a talented person and a very bright star. He was a good person who gave away a lot of money. He gave me quite a bit of money too. I won that $22,000.00 and because of that I semi retired and nobody really knew about that.

When was the last time you saw Elvis?
The last time I saw him was at the last show he did in Las Vegas and he had begun to swell quite a bit. This was 1976 and it wasn't the Elvis I knew during those shows in 1970 and it hurt me to see him like it, he just wasn't himself.

Lets close with a nice story from your years at RCA.
Well, one time when I was on night shift I got a call from Alabama and two young ladies were on the phone and they wanted to know all about Elvis. I didn't know who they were but I enjoyed talking with them. I got a letter from them two young ladies thanking me for giving them information about Elvis. They were trying to get in touch with Elvis through the company but we never gave those details out to nobody.

Lionel, thank you so much for your time and enjoy the rest of your time here in Memphis.
It was a real pleasure talking with you.

> **"** It makes me sad sometimes when
> I think back to Elvis' tragic death,
> he should still be here with us
> and I just get upset. **"**

Anita Wood

"1961 was the last time I saw Anita. We had the best time when she was around, you just can't imagine. Anita had a crazy sense of humour just like Elvis. She was just a wonderful lady and we all loved her very much. We were all disappointed when it didn't work out."
Sonny West

A dream came true for me last year when I got to meet one of Elvis' serious girlfriends, Anita Wood. Lamar Fike introduced me to Anita, who was in Memphis catching up with old friends, and she agreed to talk to me, for the first time, about her romance with Elvis. Although wedding bells almost rang for the pair, who dated seriously for several years, Anita eventually married NFL football personality Johnny Brewer. She now teaches in a Christian school in Mississippi.

Why is this the first time you've spoken about your time with Elvis?
I really don't do any interviews because it makes me sad sometimes when I think back to Elvis' tragic death, he should still be here with us and I just get upset. So, I've stayed at home in Mississippi with my husband, three children and six grandchildren.

Tell me about your first date with Elvis.
I went on to do *Dance Party* with Wink Martindale, which was a Saturday

programme for teenagers where George Klein worked. I really was not an Elvis fan before I met him but I was a disc jockey and I did play his records. Well, one particular Saturday Lamar Fike called me and said that Elvis would like to meet me and I told him that I was sorry but I already had a date for that night. I explained that I couldn't let my date down, Elvis wouldn't have liked it if it were him, and that I was very sorry.

A couple of weeks later Lamar called again and said Elvis would like a date and was I free that night. At the time I was living with a lady that I had met called Miss Patty who became a real mother figure to me and I told Lamar to ask Elvis to pick me up there and we set a time. When he came by in his Cadillac, Elvis was driving. He sent George Klein up to the door, which was a big mistake, and Miss Patty told him that she was sorry but Elvis would have to come himself if he wanted a date.

Anyway, Elvis came back with George, this was just after he had made *Loving You* and he wore a red velvet shirt and looked very, very handsome. I must say that he was the best looking man that I have ever seen. Anyway, George made the introductions to me and to Miss Patty who told them to have me back at a sensible hour or she wouldn't let me go.

I went out to the Cadillac and there was Lamar and a few other guys. We just drove around laughing and talking, having a great time. Elvis got hungry so he stopped by the store for some hamburgers.

We drove up to Graceland where I remember he had a whole lot of teddy bears in the dinning room. All of a sudden Elvis said, "I want to show you my bedroom" and so we went upstairs and he started to kiss me.

Now, this was the first date and his hands started to move where I thought they shouldn't so I said, "I think I need to go home now." He acted real nice, we went down stairs and he took me home.

And the second date?
The second date was a couple of nights later and we went up to Graceland again. You know, Elvis still had an old truck and we'd get in it and he would drive me down to Lauderdale Courts to show me where he used to live. He'd show me around Memphis and nobody would ever bother us because they really didn't recognise him in that truck. We just went back to his house, watched television, ate and had a good time. Then Elvis took me home.

How long were you with Elvis before you both felt that you were really in love with each other?
Well, I'd never really had a serious boyfriend because my parents were very strict. I wasn't allowed to go on dates and I was nineteen when I met Elvis so he was really my first one. I've always said that Elvis was my first love but Johnny is my true love. Elvis and I saw each other a lot and after about two months we were on a date and after he took mc homc wc stood on thc porch and he said, "Little, I think I'm falling in love with you." He was loving, kind and he made me laugh.

Tell us about of Elvis' army induction?
When Elvis was inducted into the army I had to go to New York for thirteen weeks to work on the Andy Williams talk show. Before this though, Elvis took me to Killeen, Texas where he was stationed. His mother wasn't feeling too good at this time and I thought the world of her. She and I often talked about the time

that Elvis would marry me and we would have a little boy and that just made her very happy. But anyway, she got real sick and Elvis called me one morning and told me of her death. I drove up to Graceland and there was Mr. Presley and Elvis sitting on the front porch and they were so sad. I couldn't really sympathise with them because at that time I didn't know what it was like to lose a parent. When I did lose my Dad, I talked to Elvis to let him know that I knew how he had felt.

After that I spent time with Elvis on base at Fort Hood with his family. Elvis looked tanned and wonderful. He had no dye on his hair, it was not a crew cut but it was cut short, he looked great. I would just go over and it was like a regular date but the guys had to be with us all the time but I love them, really. We'd go to Waco to visit friends and have a really good time.

How was it for you when Elvis left for Germany?
It was not very nice as Mrs. Presley was not there and there were lots of women and girlfriends around and I felt uneasy.

Do you remember the last thing Elvis said to you before he left?
Do I remember the last thing he said to me? Yeah, I remember, he said, "I love you, Little."

I understand Elvis bought you a 1957 Ford and a diamond friendship ring before he left?
He gave me a lot of things, but I never asked for anything because I loved him. The ring was the first thing he ever gave me and now my daughter has it and she wears it to this day. I gave the car to my brother when I got married and I gave certain toys and jewellery that he gave me to my bridesmaids. I thought that my husband would not appreciate me bringing these things into our marriage, gifts I received from another man. I would not appreciate him doing that, so I gave everything away except that little ring.

Do you have any photographs of Elvis that we haven't seen?

You know, I do have one of Elvis when he came by Miss Patty's. We were standing out front talking when the picture was taken. I do have some pictures but Elvis did not want the newspapers to know anything about how serious we were so not many photographs were taken.

Why didn't you get married?

Elvis told me that Colonel Tom Parker had said no because if he got married or engaged or anything, with that kind of career, he didn't need that kind of publicity.

How did you find out about Priscilla?

I was with Elvis when he was shooting a movie in 1962 and one time when he went to the studio I stayed at home. I was up in Elvis' room looking through some books in the library and inside one was a letter. I opened the letter and it was from Priscilla. Let me tell you, I was mad because he had not mentioned any other women. When I asked him about it he got upset and told me that it was just a love letter from some fan. We had a big fight and Elvis grabbed me and threw me up against the closet.

Things obviously became difficult from then on. How did it finally end?

One afternoon Elvis was sitting in the kitchen, I think he was with Alan Fortas, and I was on my way down the backstairs. All of a sudden I heard Elvis say, "I'm having a hard time making up my mind between them." I was hurt and I walked in and simply said, "Well, I'm going to make your mind up for you" and I left. I wasn't going to remain there in that situation. Elvis came after me and said, "I pray to God you're doing the right thing" and I told him that it didn't matter and it didn't make any difference. Elvis became upset and Mr. Presley began to cry too. Elvis was trying to put money in my purse and I just didn't know what was going on. It was very hard but I never went back.

Did you see Elvis perform in Las Vegas during the 1970s?

I went to Las Vegas with a girlfriend once and I ran into Joe Esposito, George Klein and Lamar who said, "Elvis is performing tonight. If you'll come I'll save you a seat up front." So I talked to Johnny about it who had been the night before and he had no problem with me seeing the show. So, I had a seat right there next to the stage and when Elvis walked on he looked wonderful. He saw me there and a lot of the songs he sung straight to me. When the show was over Charlie Hodge came over and told me that Elvis would like to see me backstage. I went and saw him and we hugged for a long time before he said, "Little, I wondered if we made a mistake," and I said, "No Elvis, we didn't, you wouldn't have Lisa and I wouldn't have my children and my husband." This was the last time I saw him, but I talked to him sometime later when my father died, like I told you before. I wanted to tell him that I knew what he felt when his mother died but his voice sounded so slow and deep at that time.

What's your most precious memory of Elvis?

I have a lot of good memories, but the time he gave me the friendship ring in California was special moment. He gave it to me in our hotel and it was really sweet. I was just amazed.

In closing, how about a final thought?

I just can't believe ya'll still love him so much, and I really wish he could be here now. He would be laughing with us, he had such a great sense of humour.

I still telephone Anita occasionally and we last spoke at Christmas when I called to wish her, Johnny and the family our best wishes for the festive season. I'll probably call again to see what she thinks of the magazine. Hey, If it means that I get to talk with Anita, then any excuse will do!

❝ When Elvis did his first few shows in Vegas he was in fighting condition, he looked fantastic. **❞**

Marc Bannerman

Marc Bannerman is probably most famous for his role as the fiery Italian, Gianni di Marco, in *EastEnders*. Despite Marc's convincing Italian looks, he is actually from Irish decent and was born in Dublin in 1973. Marc moved to London as a small child and has remained a Londoner since. Now twenty-seven, Marc really does have the world, and many female admirers, at his feet.

Since leaving Albert Square, Marc has starred in the hilarious comedy *Time Gentlemen Please* along side Julia Sawahla. With a schedule more packed than the Fowler's fruit stall, he is currently working on a film, based around his first love of boxing.

Polly Hearn caught up with Elvis fan Marc during his stint as pantomime baddie, King Rat, in *Dick Whittington* [Oh yes she did!]. Just like every other Elvis fan, Marc's voice gets quicker and more excitable as he talks about Elvis. It is clear that it is more a case of King Elvis than Queen Vic as far as he' is concerned!

Many Elvis fans will have seen Marc's performance on *Stars in their Eyes* as Elvis. Although keen to ask him about the infamous black leather outfit, I started by asking how he first became interested in Elvis.
I tell you what; my mum was fascinated by Elvis for as long as I can remember. She used to have all his pictures on the wall and loads of videos and stuff. She used to listen to all the old stuff like *Teddy Bear* and *All Shook Up*, which I quite liked at the time. Then, just after my 4th birthday, he died and my Mum was in tears. People were upset and I wanted to know why. She told me Elvis was dead and I can still remember clearly hearing on the radio that Elvis Presley had died. The whole country was in shock.

So, although you were very young, you can clearly remember when Elvis died?
I can yeah, especially the bit on the radio. I wanted to find out more about it. If everyone was so upset about this guy dying, then he must be someone really special. I'm a bit of an old fuddy-duddy really. I'm not up with the latest chart stuff or new music. I went to live with my dad when I was five and he was always into the old boys like Chubby Checker and Fats Domino. So, I got into the Everly Brothers and rock 'n' roll, but Elvis, he was cool, man - he was a cool cat for me. I got into the Beatles too, Tom Jones I didn't get into until later.

Did the other kids at school ever make fun of you for liking Elvis, or call you square?
No, no one ever picked on me or called me square - I wouldn't stand for it. I do exactly what I want when I please. If I want to like Elvis and someone wants to say something about it, then I would, as Frank Butcher would say, I'd give 'em a dry slap! In my opinion, there is nothing square about Elvis. I don't understand all the youngsters today driving around bashing their heads to garage - it's music with no soul.

Why was Elvis the coolest cat for you?
You know, as I grew up, I started reading all these stories about his life and the sadness. I believe that the emotional hold that his mother had over him led to a lot of his sadness. I felt quite sorry for the fella, but you couldn't feel sorry for him, because in his own world, he was just taking care of business. And he was so cool, with his moves, and his rhythm, and his voice. You can hear the pain in his voice and you can hear the laughter in his voice - it just fascinated me. I've read books and they talk about relationships with younger girls and all that, but I just think, to me, he wanted to give them a little bit of love or, maybe he saw something in them that he missed as a child. You know, with his over-bearing mother and his hopeless drunk of a father, he wanted to give them a little bit of love and that's what he did - probably just talking and cuddles.

The music is of course only half the story; do you like Elvis' films?
Er, no, I don't like his films. I watch them because Elvis is in them, but not really. I like *King Creole* and I like *Jailhouse Rock*. Those two were quite good films, you felt they were really real, especially *King Creole*. The other films, I think he sold himself short, but then he knew what he was doing and he needed the money because he was a generous fella and he needed money generated. Colonel Tom Parker obviously had a big slice of the action and Elvis was misguided. He had no-one to teach him and tell him what was right and what was wrong. He always remained quite young, I feel, and he was taken into this world, where he became King. So, I think he did sell himself a bit short, but then he was so good looking it doesn't really matter, does it?

After the films, Elvis famously returned with the 1968 TV special, which you took off, when you appeared in the celebrity version of *Stars in their Eyes*. How did it feel when you said those immortal words 'Tonight Matthew, I'm going to be Elvis Presley'?
My then girlfriend Nadia and my agent, who thought it would be a good idea for me to do Elvis, roped me into doing *Stars In Their Eyes*. Before, I'd done a bit of an Elvis impersonation, but I had never thought of singing in front of people. Maybe karaoke or a family wedding or something like that. But they (*Stars In their Eyes*) got wind of it and they kept pushing my agent and Nadia to set up a meeting.

So, I went along and basically, the meeting was to discuss what costume I'd be wearing and what song I would be singing. I didn't know that, I thought I was just there for a chat. So anyway, that happened and then I had about three months before I had to do it. I never planned to go through with it, I was always going to pull out, but when it came to it, I just couldn't. I'd had a couple of singing lessons, but I really terrified myself and I couldn't hear the words "Tonight Matthew...". It did give me an excuse to check out Elvis' moves again and watch his concerts. I spent about three months watching Elvis all day, because I was 'researching' - lovely!' Anyway, the Saturday morning came and I put my Elvis outfit on and I'm being really, really cocky. I was over cocky really, trying to make it look like I wasn't nervous. Then come the time when I'm wanted on stage (for rehearsals), the music started. It was pony ('pony and trap' - cockney rhyming slang for crap! - PH) music man, nothing like it. I would have preferred one of Elvis' live concert backings, but it was a slowed down version. I had no idea what I was doing, but I was so terrified I blocked it out and I didn't talk to anyone about it. I should have done really - story of my life! I'd backed myself up against a wall and I had to do it. Anyway, it came to the actual show and all that confidence went out window and I could have easily gone to pieces. Nadia had helped me out a lot that day. She worked with me on it over and over again, helping me with where to come in and with my moves and stuff - thank God she did. I got such a buzz, such a rush when I did it.

Nadia was in the audience; did that help you at all with the final performance?
Yeah, Nadia was there. To be honest though, I work better without people I know there; well actually, I'm not sure. I get a bit nervous when there are people I know watching, but when it's people I don't know, I don't give a monkey's. On reflection, I think it did help that Nadia was there.

With Nadia helping you out so much - is she a fan?
Of me? Yeah she's a massive fan of me. She really is, she's my biggest fan!

And of Elvis?
Is she a fan of Elvis? She is yeah. More so than she would let you believe. I don't think she was before she met me, but now she is a massive fan.

Have you watched the show back?
Yeah, my Dad's got a copy. He's another one of my biggest fans. I don't think I particularly sounded too much like Elvis; I just felt I was a little bit insecure. I put in a couple of cheeky moves - hopefully not too much. If there are any Elvis fans out there that didn't like what I did, then fair enough, but I just wanted to do something to show my appreciation of Elvis and his music. I had a great time doing it and I hope it wasn't that bad. *Stars In Their Eyes* sent me a tape of an entire Elvis show they had done a few years ago. Some of them boys were terrible - it's a mockery.

Did they let you keep the outfit?
Yeah, £2,000 that cost and it still fits. In fact, I've lost a lot of weight.

You were quite open with your weight loss despite being in the public eye; can you sympathise with Elvis' weight gain?
Well, I put on over two stone. I can hold it quite well, but when you go over those speed bumps and your belly hits your belt, then I thought 'No, I'm not having that anymore - it's not me.' You know, I don't want to feel embarrassed to take my top off. I think Elvis was comfort eating really and the same with me. I was going through a bit of a funny time and some big changes in my life. I come from a very poor family and then all of a sudden I'm in the public eye and I've got a bit of pressure. You know, I'd never really felt pressure before; I'd always been a bit of a free spirit. I was boozing a little bit, 'cos I was shy going out, you know, it just gets a bit difficult sometimes.

From humble beginnings to a life of fame and fortune - sounds familiar?

Yeah, my dad was a truck driver too, but my similarity with Elvis stops there! When starring in the pantomime, you are doing two shows a day, seven days a week. Although only for three weeks, it's similar to Elvis' Vegas commitments.

How tough have you found the schedule?

Easy! But, I've got a lot of energy and I mean a lot of energy. But then, if it were for a longer time, I wouldn't do it. I like doing TV work really. I like working with the camera. I mean panto, it's a joke, it's a bit of fun - it's not my thing. I struggled in rehearsals. The rest of the cast, they're all panto people and they all do it regularly.

So this is your first pantomime?

Yeah, I'd never even seen one before. I was a very unfortunate child!

Would you do it again?

No! But I love playing a baddie. I always play a baddie. I love it 'cos you can go out on stage and have a real slanging match. Then you can just wipe off your make-up and go home. You release a lot of aggression playing a baddie - who wants to be a goodie?

Do you have any other idols?

I don't really have idols. Elvis isn't an idol. I just have people I admire and appreciate. Anyone who's got a bit of fun, talent and confidence, and who doesn't apologise for it.

Is there anyone around at the moment that fits that description?

I think Robbie Williams is a great entertainer. He shows that people have still got what it takes. Apart from that, I like David Gray too. I find a lot of pop music pony nowadays. It's lost its sense of entertainment; it's too plastic. You know, I've never really understood idols. I don't know why someone would want my signature on a bit of paper, but if people like what I do, then great.

So, do you get a lot of underwear sent through the post with fan mail?

I did when I first started on *EastEnders*. I used to get nude pictures and all kind of things, but then they realised I wasn't that kind of person. I mean, I don't appreciate girls that flaunt it. I've just got on with my job really.

If Hollywood were to approach you to play Elvis in a movie of his life, would you consider the part?

Kurt Russell's done quite a good job of that already, but there have been some pony ones too. I saw an Elvis movie with Don Johnson on satellite the other day. That was outrageous - he should be shot! But yeah, I would definitely like to give it a go. When I was at drama school, they were bringing out *Elvis - The Musical*. I was just starting my second year and I saw the advert in *The Stage* and did stop and think for a moment.

The musical is brought back every now and then, would you consider doing it now?

Well, the thing is, Elvis' voice is much higher than mine so there are only a couple of songs I could sing.

What era would you like to portray?

Well, I just love the Vegas years. When he did his first few shows in Vegas he was in fighting condition, he looked fantastic. I think he just got lonely. I mean he was obviously on quite a few drugs, but then his mum was on amphetamines when he was growing up.

What do you think about the drugs?

I think he did it to escape. He didn't feel he deserved everything he had. He was as insecure as anyone else. As a performer, he felt he couldn't be the person that people thought he was. No one can believe that they are that great or that they are the King, or that the world revolves around them, the man

was just normal. You've got to admire him. I mean, he did his time in the army when he could have easily got out of it. He mucked in and I think he enjoyed the camaraderie.

Have you ever visited Graceland?
No, but *Wish You Were Here*, the holiday programme, have approached me about doing a show from Graceland. I'd love to do that, so hopefully it will happen.

What will you look forward to seeing the most?
Just the house generally and seeing how he lived. It's all done out how it was in the '70s isn't it? I grew up on a council estate and all the people on the estate knew, it was their own little world. The local pub, the local shops, I think Elvis was the same. All he really knew was Graceland and Memphis. It all

happened for him at such a young age, I don't think he really had any choice, but to stay there.

And finally, how do you think Elvis should be remembered?
Well, I just think the way he is remembered, as a fantastic entertainer, a generous man, very good looking with a gift. He defies all logic. To be given his fame, his looks, his voice and his natural ability, I don't think he could have gone any other way. The fact that he died early just adds to that.

Marc, it's been an absolute pleasure talking to you. Thanks for your time and good luck for everything you do in the future.

In my opinion, definitely more of a Prince Charming, than a King Rat!

"Elvis was just unique, incredibly sensual and tender. He was funny and he was good. He was an extreme in every aspect of his life."

Linda Thompson

Can you start by telling me a little about how your first meeting with Elvis was set up? I believe an RCA guy called Bill Browder was responsible?
Yes, I knew him as Bill Browder but he actually became TG Sheppard who later became a country artist who did a song called *Devil in a Bottle*, and he had a lot of success with it. I was Miss Tennessee at the time and my girlfriend, who was my roommate in the Miss USA pageant, was a girl named Jeanne LeMay. She was Miss Rhode Island and had just moved to Memphis. Anyway, we were out walking one day and she suggested we go into Fridays and have some lunch. So we walk into Fridays and Bill Browder is there and he asks if we'd like to join him for lunch. He then asks us if we'd like to meet Elvis as he was in town. If it had not been for Jeanne, I probably would not have met him because I was very conservative and I was about to say that we were busy because we were both supposed to model that night. Jeanne said that we would meet him and that we'd cancel our plans.

Were you an Elvis fan at this time?
Oh yes, I had been my whole life but I knew that we had this modelling job to do and I was happy to stick with my commitment but Jeanne said that if there was an opportunity to meet Elvis, she was going to take it. So, we cancelled our modelling engagement and they got

replacements for us. We went to the Memphian Theatre at midnight because that's when it closed and Elvis took over and showed movies.

What was he like? What was your first impression of him?
Well, I was in the lobby talking to some of the guys and a few of the people who were hanging around there and the door burst open and there was this vision. It was the middle of July in Memphis and it was very humid, just sweltering. He had on this black cape with a high collar and a red satin lining and I said "Dressed a little like Dracula aren't we?" So you see, we both shared a sense of humour that was very much like the other. We just hit it off immediately because we grew up in Memphis, we had the same religious beliefs, the same love for our family, devotion to mother and father. We had the same sense of loyalty; we enjoyed the same cuisine because we were both Southerners.

It sounds like it was almost inevitable?
Oh, it was. We shared a real kinship. I mean, we became kindred souls. So much so that he said, "Where have you been?" and I said "Growing up!"

He had just split from Priscilla when you two first met right?
It's funny because when we met at the Memphian Theatre, he was telling me that he'd just separated. We met on July 6th and he had been separated since the beginning of January.

came around and said hi. We started talking and we became really close. I loved being with her. You know, Elvis had a real childlike spirit and I have too. I like to do childlike things and to sometimes get down to a child's level. She and I became very close.

Are you still close with her now?
Yes, I am.

I believe it was Lisa who told you of Elvis' death?
She called me. She was only nine-years-old but she had the presence of mind to call me and tell me what had happened.

Was it really a shock to you or could you see that it was going to happen?
You know, even if someone that you know is on a destructive path, even when they finally pass away, it's always shocking. Yes, it was a shock.

You saved his life once or twice right?
Yes, a few times.

Did you both ever discuss marriage?
We talked about marriage often. We talked about having children too. When Elvis was in the hospital a couple of times with pneumonia and other health problems, I stayed in the hospital with him for two and a half weeks at a time. I had my own hospital bed that was pushed up against his. I even ate hospital food. I was a young, healthy, vibrant girl but I'm in a hospital bed pressing the buttons to move up and down in tandem with him. The TV would go off at night, we didn't have all-night cable like we do now, and we'd turn the monitor to the nursery and pick out the different babies that

> **"** *Elvis had such an amazingly wonderful sense of humour. If you can laugh with someone then you can spend a lot of years with them.* **"**

You obviously met Lisa Marie pretty soon after you began dating. How quick did she accept you as her father's new partner?
She was a wonderful little girl. She was very embracing and a little shy but I've always loved children and we got on really well. The first time I ever saw her was at the Monovale house and I was out by the pool. She kind of timidly

we'd like to have (laughs).

So Elvis had CCTV in his room? Was it something he requested?
We had a television in the room that you could switch over to the nursery. I don't think Elvis requested it but for privacy, we were put near the floor where the babies were.

What about the guys that were around Elvis? Did you get along with all of them?
We actually got along very well and I remain friendly with a number of them now.

Was there anyone in particular that you were able to share the difficult times with? David Brigg's (Elvis' piano player) became a close friend didn't he?
Actually, we shared a romantic relationship for over two-and-a-half years and we remain friends as well. You see, in all honesty, there was no way of really meeting anybody. It was Elvis' world and we lived this kind of reversed life where we were awake all night and asleep all day. I was around the same people all the time so it was natural that when I left, a gravitated to someone who I had been close to and shared things with. We both had a common love of Elvis too. We both loved him very much and found it sad to watch him self-destruct.

Were you in contact with Elvis between the time that you left and when he died?
Well, he died only eight months after I left. We did speak once or twice because I worried about him and I would call. I called Graceland a couple of times just to see how he was because I was worried. I asked Charlie Hodge or Ricky Stanley, or whoever was attending to him, to please go and check on him. They would insist that he was fine but I'd ask them to put me on hold, go up and check, and let me know he's okay. I did that several times without speaking to him but I did speak to him a couple

of times too. We were very loving with each other and... we loved each other. I know that Elvis understood my heart and I really loved him dearly.

I know that's true. I have just one difficult question. If you were still with him in August 1977, do you think you would have been there to perhaps save his life?
Well, I know that I've had a past record of having saved his life several times when certain things happened and you're right, it's a difficult one because everybody around him, including his father, had said that if I'd have been with him he would have still been alive. His father told me that on the night of the funeral. All of his friends and relatives have said that to me too. That is something that we will now never know. I could have stayed there and kept him alive for another ten years or I might have found him dead the same way that Ginger did. That would have been even more devastating to me than the fact that I could have been there or I might have done something. I think God has a way of working things out. He removed me from the situation because maybe there was nothing I could've done.

It's impossible for any of us to change the course of history.
Exactly.

Can I just check a story with you? It's something that was supposed to have happened and it's such a great story that I kind of hope it did. You and Elvis were eating in McDonalds and someone thought he was an impersonator...
The story is true but the details are a little wrong. We never ate in McDonalds. We were approaching the Memphian Theatre where I told you that at midnight we went to see movies. We were walking in and he was slightly ahead of me and someone came up to him and said, "Oh my God, look, it's Elvis. You're Elvis aren't you?" He said, "Well, yes, I am Elvis" and they went crazy. They wanted an autograph and a

picture. As I walked up I said, "Charlie, you're not using that Elvis bit again are you? Come on, you're not telling these people that you're Elvis again are you?" I told the fans, "He gets it all the time and he's always messing with people." The fans said, "We knew you couldn't really be Elvis" and he replied, "But I am, tell 'em honey!" I replied, "Come on Charlie, we're late."

That sounds like it was fun.
He had such an amazingly wonderful sense of humour and we shared that. If you can laugh with someone then you can spend a lot of years with them. You can forgive a lot of things; overlook a lot of things.

Do you remember Elvis' poem about the robin that he told at your brother Sam's house in Memphis during an intimate 1974 jam?
Is that out?

It's out on CD and I can send you a copy if you'd like to hear it again.
Would you? RCA tried to buy that from me and I said no. It's bootlegged I guess but it's okay. I'd love to hear it. My children were asking about it just the other day and I was looking for my tape. I have it on a little cassette tape somewhere. As I awoke this morning, when all sweet things are born, A robin perched upon my windowsill to greet the coming morn... that's the poem right?

That's the one. You can finish it if you like (laughs).
He sang his song so sweetly, and paused for a moment's lull. I gently raised the window, and crushing his *bleeping* skull (laughs).

You know it off by heart, but you left out the swear word!
(Laughs). That was his favourite poem.

Have you ever met anyone with as much charisma as Elvis?
I don't ever expect to meet anyone again

in my life with that absolute magic. Elvis was one of a kind. He was a mould-breaker. My grandmother used to say that he broke the mould.

Do you still have your TLC - Tender Loving Care - necklace?
Oh yeah, I still have it and I still wear it occasionally. Not to take away from anyone else that I've loved in my life. Everyone has a personal magic. We're all like snowflakes, unique in our creation. We're so much alike and we're all just drifting through life but we all have our own character, our own shape. Elvis was just unique, incredibly sensual and tender. He was funny and he was good. He was an extreme in every aspect of his life.

What about the time when he only just missed you with a bullet in Las Vegas?
He was just like a little child. It's astounding when you think about the guns that he had because I'm so aware now of gun control and the danger of handguns. When I look back and think about when he had guns around that were loaded and a young child around. You know, we just said to Lisa to never go near the guns and she didn't. But who knows, if she had been a more disobedient child or a more curious child, it's astounding. It makes my blood run cold when I think about the responsibility.

It's a miracle that nobody was killed or injured but I think the incident with you was the nearest right?
That's right. I'd just happened to have come out of the shower at the Las Vegas Hilton, the presidential suite, and he was lying on the sofa. In those days they had these huge bull's eye advertisements. Vegas came alive when Elvis was there and they had these billboards, posters and placards. So he had one of these enormous bull's eye things in the suite and he decided that he would just shoot for the target. It was a kind of cardboard cut-out of his

said that it was just Elvis having a little target practice. I threw my robe on, put a towel around my head and went outside and said, "What do you think you are doing? You almost shot me!" and he went white. It was as though someone had told him that the bullet had gone through the wall and that I was hit. He couldn't even get up because he was so shaken.

Well, that's the child in him that you just mentioned. He was being scorned.
I know, I was scolding him and he just shrivelled. He said, "Oh my God, I didn't know you were in there. I didn't know it would go through the wall. I thought it would just lodge there." I said, "You could have killed me!" and he asked if I wanted to go home. I said, "Well, at least I won't get shot at there!" He was profusely apologetic but he was really shaken up. He was ashen.

That bullet story is in the film *Elvis and the Beauty Queen*. What did you think of the movie?
You know, it was a little frustrating because it's impossible to encapsulate in two hours what happened in a five-year relationship of the intensity of my relationship with Elvis. It's difficult to be totally objective about it because it was so close to everything that happened. I felt that they chose something to expound upon like the drug usage and such problems more than his sensitivity, his generosity, his playfulness and his talent. You know, these are the things that I talked in length about. I spoke far more in detail about the acts of generosity and his spirituality and his kindness. Of course there was the drug abuse and the self-destructiveness, but this is what they expounded upon. I felt

name with this bull's eye... like hit the mark, come see Elvis... whatever. So, Elvis pulled out his gun and shot at the bull's eye and the bullet went through the wall, which was adjacent to my bathroom. It went through the wall, then through the toilet paper holder, which was metal, out through a mirrored door and shattered it. I was standing at the sink and I heard ting, ting, and the sound of glass breaking. I felt the air behind my leg. When I looked down there was a bullet hole in the door behind me. I opened that door and there was another shattered glass door and a bullet lying there.

I knew exactly what was happening. James Caughley came in and said, "Linda, are you okay?" and I said, "Yeah, what the hell was that?" and he that it was more of a personal slant for the writer but they couldn't have been nicer and kinder to me and it couldn't have been any more flattering to me, which I appreciated. I'm sorry that more of his goodness didn't show in the movie. There was so much. It should have been a mini-series and people should have come away thinking 'my God what an incredible human being he was, flawed and troubled yes, but what a phenomenal, incredible human being.'

How would you like to finish this interview?
I should probably tell you this; the years I was with Elvis, I'd always been a poet. I was baptised when I was nine years old at the Baptist Church in Memphis and I've always felt that the gift that God gave me was to write poetry. So, I started when I was nine years old and I wrote poetry for my father, my mother and all my family. That's how I started writing lyrics and when I was with Elvis I would write love poems. You know, if he ever hurt me I would write that out and express to him everything through poetry. He would always say, "Honey, this is beautiful, won't you let me have someone put this to music and I'll record it because it's so pretty?" and I would always say no because I felt it was personal. And now, in my stupidity, I had no idea about royalties (laughs) but I know that when he died, he knew that I wasn't there for any other reason, any commercial consideration or anything. I was there only because I truly loved him.

You can't put a price on your memories or what you have in your heart.
That's right, but I think that he would get a real kick out of the fact that I've become a successful songwriter and that I am able to bring all that poetry to song. Having records cut and stuff.

Absolutely, I was so surprised to learn that you'd written hits for Whitney Houston and Celine Dion.
David's musicality would have been a big source of joy for Elvis too. Elvis loved

musicians. He loved David Briggs, he loved his music, so I'm sure he'd really appreciate my husband's music.

I know that he appreciated you, and fans throughout the world are aware of that.
That's been such a great source of comfort to me, to feel that love shared throughout the world. All fan magazines and tabloids have always dealt with me very kindly. I really take more satisfaction in that than anything. Knowing that people really understand how much I loved Elvis. The people who love him appreciate that and they let me know it.

Do you have any unseen photographs of you and Elvis together? It's so hard to find any good clear shots.
You know why? Because we never allowed any photographs to be taken. I respected that about his privacy and he was very skittish about people taking photographs, so there aren't all that many of us together.

I've seen several good photographs of you in the 1970s. You have very long eyelashes don't you Linda!
(Laughs) I do don't I? My children have those too. In my family on my mother's side, everybody has long eyelashes. People used to think that I wore false eyelashes but I never did.

Well, I hope you like the photos we choose to go with the interview when it's printed.
Oh I'm sure I will and thank all the fans for remaining loyal and devoted to Elvis.

I will and I'm sure they'll say the same to you. Thanks for allowing us your first ever Elvis magazine interview.
Okay. Keep up the good work and we'll be in touch.

❝I remember sitting in Elvis suite. It was pink with a round bed and to me it was beautiful. It was beautiful in those days but today I'd probably laugh at it.❞

Barbara Leigh

Barbara Leigh was born in Tennessee and lived in Georgia until the age of five when she moved with her family to Miami, Florida. At the age of sixteen, she went back to Georgia for a summer vacation where she met her first love and ended up staying there to marry. Three years later, Barbara and her family moved to Los Angeles where she began to work as a nurse, raising her small son. She was soon divorced and living the life of a single mother.

A co-worker asked if she would like to visit Beverly Hills and go dancing at The Other Place, a popular nightclub that no longer exists. That evening, singer Mark Devlin spotted her in the audience and went to her table after the show had finished. They began dating and shortly after that, he had professional photographs taken of her, which were later sold to Kodak Film. This was the beginning of her modelling career.

Her agent became Dick Clayton, who was well known for discovering James Dean, amongst other major celebrities. It was a great break for Barbara to have been signed by him. She began to study acting with Charles Conrad, and also signed with Ashley Famous for commercials. Her first commercial effort was for Coca-Cola.

When she joined the Screen Actors Guild, her married name Barbara Haynes had already been taken, bringing about the need for a change. One of her agents who happened to be reading that Vivian Leigh had died, abruptly blurted out to the whole office, "That's it, Barbara Leigh!" Vivian Leigh died and Barbara Leigh was born.

Barbara went on to make nearly fifty commercials, several of which won awards for Best Commercial of the Year. She began making films and appearing in television movies too.

She was then seen walking on the beach in Malibu by French director Roger Vadim, who is famous for discovering Bridgette Bardot. Running from his beach front home, he asked if she would like to audition for the role of Jean, Rock Hudson's wife in the movie *Pretty Maids All In A Row*.

Barbara found Hudson to be one of the nicest and most generous people in Hollywood. Barbara says of Rock, "If he found out I was in the studio he'd come to visit regardless of which set I was on. Rock Hudson made me feel very special. He was a wonderful man, and I miss him a lot."

Barbara went on to make successful movies with some fine actors like Tom Selleck and Steve McQueen who she seriously dated. Barbara has also modelled around the world, gracing the covers of dozens of magazines. She currently works for Playboy magazine and has done two celebrity pictorials (May 1973 and January 1977). In her spare time, Barbara works with Animal Rescue as a hobby and volunteers her time to the AIDS Health Care Foundation, as well as the Starlight Foundation.

Barbara also dated the President of MGM Studios, the legendary James T. Aubrey (known as the Smiling Cobra and The Love Machine). It was James who introduced Barbara to Elvis after one of his shows at the Las Vegas Hilton and they soon began dating.

There's a biography out too. *The King, McQueen and The Love Machine* has been written with the help of well-known autobiographer Marshall Terrill. The book is about Barbara's life and details the excitement, passion and heartache of her extraordinary romantic relationships with Elvis, Steve McQueen and James Aubrey.

I understand you were dating James Aubrey, the head of MGM, when you first met Elvis in the summer of 1970.

I was and we actually went to Las Vegas to see Elvis' show. James Aubrey (Everyone called him Jim but I always called him James) asked me if I wanted to go and see Elvis and I was like "Oh my God" but I was with James so I didn't let on to just how excited I really was. I adored Elvis so it was really exciting to know that I was going to see him. I never even thought about having the opportunity of meeting him let alone see him perform. So that was very exciting.

When did your initial meeting with Elvis actually take place?

That was after the show. Joe Esposito came to our table to invite us backstage to meet Elvis. I guess Joe had seen us and maybe told Elvis about me. I had the look he liked in a woman like long, straight dark hair and a lot of eye make-up. I remember the dress I was wearing too. It was black with spaghetti straps that criss-crossed at the front and tied down at the waist. It was a pretty smashing dress. I was really tanned and I didn't wear a lot of jewellery. Also, I was vulnerable and he liked vulnerable women.

So, it was Joe that spotted you?
Joe saw me and said to Elvis, "Wait 'till you see the girl James Aubrey' is with."

James was a bit of a casanova right?
He was a casanova, but so was Elvis and so was Steve McQueen (laughs).

How did the meeting go?
What happened is this: We were invited backstage and I was so excited that I could hardly hide it. I was trying to be very cool in front of James because I didn't want him to know how much I adored Elvis.

Would he have been angry?
Well, not angry but perhaps jealous. So, we actually went to Elvis' private dressing room but he wasn't around because he was still changing. In the centre of the room was a large round table so we sat down. There were a lot of other people around and I started talking to Chris Nelson who was married to the singer Ricky Nelson. My back was facing the door that Elvis finally came out of but I just felt this presence. I really wasn't paying any attention, just kind of looking around the room. I felt someone looking at me so I turned by chair around and Elvis was sitting down and staring directly into my eyes. His vision never once left mine. Once he sat down, his gaze never altered. It was like he never looked at anyone else in the room. He started off by asking me my name and because I still had a little bit of a Southern accent, he asked me where I was from. I told him I was from Georgia and he said that he loved Georgia girls. We got along really well and I felt so comfortable with him from the moment I met him.

It would be pretty safe to say that your first impression of him was a good one then?
I felt he was a real Southern gentleman and he actually had a vulnerability about him too. Elvis was very attentive to the current woman in his life so you felt like you were the only one, even if you weren't. He could just melt anybody with his smile. It was so wonderful, kind of like a crooked bad-boy smile. When he smiled it lit up the world.

Just so I can build a full picture. Can you remember what he was wearing?
I honestly can't, but when he wasn't performing his standard dress was a high-collared shirt with kind of puffy sleeves. He wore black slacks a lot and he looked very sexy. He was thin and gorgeous.

All this happened around the time of *That's The Way It Is* right?
Yes, that's why we were there, because James was involved in the movie. It was August or maybe September because I think it was Labour Day about a week after we met. I love that movie because it shows his vulnerability when he's messing around with the guys. Elvis was a big kidder. He liked to tease, tell jokes and sometimes make fun of people. Sometimes people could get hurt because they were at the brunt of it.

I think Lamar Fike got most it.
Yeah, he made fun of Lamar a lot.

Going back to the meeting, where was James when you were talking to Elvis?
He was over the other side of the room at the bar talking to Ricky. I felt that if the world stopped that night, it was okay because I did what I wanted to do. The first time I saw Elvis I was in eighth grade and he was on the Ed Sullivan show. He was dancing and doing all those moves and I remember getting up off the floor, standing up and trying to copy him. My parents sent me to my room for doing it. I always loved him and I never forgot him but I didn't have the freedom or ability to be a big Elvis fan, but I would've been the biggest. Anyway, after we'd talked for a while he said that he'd really like to see me again and that he'd like me to come up to see another show... without James (laughs). I was flattered and of course, I wanted to

see him again. Elvis was very prepared and I guess the minute Joe mentioned me he was going to make a play for me. Not everything was about the way I looked though; some of it was to do with his ego. It was also about competing with James. Elvis looked up to him a lot and James adored Elvis too.

How did you feel about the fact Elvis was always seeing other women besides you?
Elvis just had something about him. You know, he cheated on his wife and he had all kinds of affairs but still he had that innocence about him. You see, he was the King and you can't expect a man like that to be faithful to just one person. It just isn't going to happen. It was just the way he was. He had to have a woman by his side every second of the day. They had to wait on him hand and foot too.

It's not really accepted in this day and age but do you think that was just a Southern thing?
Well, I grew up that way and I think it might've been. I think a woman today simply wouldn't put up with it but a man would still love it. Who doesn't want to be looked after and taken care of? Today, if a man asks a woman to get him a glass of water most would tell him to get it himself. If Elvis asked me I was up and back before he knew it. Whatever he wanted he got.
Going back to the story (laughs), Elvis had a tiny little pen and a small piece of paper and he asked me if I could jot my phone number on it.

He had it all ready?
He had it ready when he sat down. He had a direction, a goal, and he achieved it. I took the pen and paper from underneath the table and I remember touching his fingers. A chill went through me as he pressed them into my hand. He also gave my hand a gentle squeeze. He was just flirting and it was very simple and sweet. I wrote down my number and handed it back to him. It all happened so quickly. Just minutes after

that, James came over to the table. He was crazy about me and he never called me Barbara, he only ever called me Indian. He put his hand on my shoulder and told me that it was time to go.

Did he call you Indian because of your background?
I do have some Indian blood in me but the look was really big in those days. I had long black hair parted in the middle and I just had that look. When James first met me he said that I looked like an Indian princess. Anyway, he said we had to go and that ended the special moment between Elvis and myself. Elvis was very courteous and he spoke with James for a few minutes. We left and I guess Elvis started socialising with the other people there.

Did James have any kind of notion about how you and Elvis felt about each other?
He knew and he was absolutely livid. He was livid because he knew Elvis was attracted to me and that I was attracted to him and he was jealous.

Did Elvis call?
On the Sunday we got back to LA and we were going to a party on Malibu beach that night. As I was pulling up into my driveway I heard the phone ringing. I dashed into my apartment and answered it and it was Elvis. We starting talking, and he wanted to know when I could go back to met him and see the show. I was working and so I couldn't think of an immediate time but he was very persistent. He asked why I couldn't go on the following weekend and I told him that it was because James and I had a boat trip planned. He suggested that I went out on Thursday and stay for the night. I said okay.
I had a Porsche convertible at the time and all of a sudden I remembered my suitcase. I ran out there and of course, it had been stolen. I lost my little black dress, what little jewellery I had and all my good stuff.

I had to find another dress to wear for meeting Elvis. He had good taste and loud taste too. I told James I was going camping and that I'd be back in time for our trip. I took the best dress I had and I went to see Elvis.

Were you modelling at this time?
I was an actress. I was in the process of shooting *Pretty Maids All In A Row* with Rock Hudson. I also did modelling and I made a good living.

You drove from LA to Vegas?
No I didn't. Elvis had Joe arrange to fly me in. I was picked up at the airport and when I got to the hotel, Joe came out and told me that I couldn't attend the first show because James had shown up with another girl.

So, he was playing the same game?
Well, he was better at it than me (laughs). I was very naive and I was really hurt. I knew I was there to see Elvis but somehow that was understandable because he was the King. But I was madly in love with James too.

I remember sitting in Elvis suite. It was pink with a round bed and to me it was beautiful. It was beautiful in those days but today I'd probably laugh at it. I sat drinking Coca-Cola from the mini bar and waited. They came and fetched me to see the second show, which I did and I got to be with Elvis afterwards. He gave me a big hug and a kiss and I was in heaven. We stayed in his room and got to know each other.

I'm sure Elvis pushed for you to stay longer didn't he?
He hated the dress I was wearing and he wanted me to stay for the weekend, but I was worried about James. He played on the fact that he'd lied to me and he told me to teach him a lesson. I didn't have any clothes because of my case and I was only expecting to be there one night. I didn't have any idea. I certainly wasn't being presumptuous so I didn't

come prepared. To cut a long story short, he worked on me and I finally gave in. He had the guys arrange for me to go shopping to buy some dresses. I think the first night I just bought something in the hotel but the following day he had Charlie (Hodge) take me to Suzy Cream Cheese, which was a really well run place in those days. I loved blue jeans but Elvis hated them. He said that jeans should only be worn when milking a cow.

I don't think he really liked to see women in jeans or trousers at all did he?
No, he liked things to be feminine. Flowing, flowery and lacy. He liked that kind of stuff.

Do you think Elvis felt that he had one up on James?
James was known, as the smiling cobra and this was his reputation and Elvis knew all about him. A mongoose can kill a cobra and somebody found him a real stuffed mongoose with a dead cobra in his mouth. Elvis loved it and he was proud of it because he felt that he had stolen James's girl and won the prize. He had a laugh with that stuffed thing. I thought it was disgusting because I love all kinds of creatures and I don't like to see them killed or tortured then stuffed and mounted on a piece of board. That was the way it was but Elvis hollered. It was the mongoose that killed the cobra.

Did you end up staying longer than the weekend?
No, I had a great weekend but it was time to go. I had work on Monday anyway. I went back to LA and I had a long phone message from James because I totally screwed up our weekend. The boat was ready and everything. I was doing it to teach him a lesson because he'd lied to me and I felt that my life wasn't as important as his. Of course, it was different for me because anyone would want to go to meet Elvis but he took another girl to

Vegas. I went out to his house and he asked me what happened. I told him that I went to see Elvis and I said that I lied but he lied to me too. I was so angry but we finally made up because I think he felt that if he had been a woman, he would've probably done the same thing. How many people get the chance to meet Elvis Presley, get to see his show and then stay with him for the weekend?

You carried on seeing Elvis after all this, even though you stayed with James?
We saw each other as often as we could after that. Through all the time I was seeing Elvis, Joe Esposito took great care of me. I love Joe and the reason we've stayed good friends is because even after Elvis died he still contacted me. It wasn't easy to snap our schedules together because we were always working. When he wanted to see me I was working and it was the same the other way around.

One of Joe's girlfriends caused a problem one time on tour didn't she?
I spent time with him [Elvis] on the road and we were in Mobile, Alabama. The girl Joe was seeing really wanted to be with Elvis and you can't blame her for that. She started saying horrible things to me like Elvis didn't really care and that he was just using me. She kept saying that he had other girlfriends but he made me feel like I was the only one and I really didn't know that he did have at least a billion other women besides me. Although I was actually doing the same to James, I found her comments hurtful and I got really depressed. I didn't say anything to Elvis but we went into his bedroom at the end of the evening and he made me tell him what was up. He got so mad that he grabbed me and dragged me down the hallway to Joe's room. He pounded on the door until Joe answered. Elvis said that he wanted to talk to his girlfriend to find out what she had said. I felt really awful because I really didn't want to get

anybody in trouble. I went in the bathroom to find her and there she was... putting on her eyelashes! That did it for me. I realised that she was only saying these things about Elvis because she wanted him. Joe laughs about it now but Elvis gave him hell over it. The girl apologised and we went back to our room.

Was Elvis still angry?
Not really, because it was then that he wrote me a little note. It was on a napkin and he wrote that he'd love me forever and he signed it from the Panther. He liked to call himself that. He jokingly wrote BLT - that showed his sense of humour.

BLT because of your initials and the bacon, lettuce and tomato sandwich right?
Right.

Any unseen photos in your collection?
Elvis and I dated for some time but I was always respectful. I never took a camera like certain people did. Joyce Bova was smart. She wasn't an actress or a model but she took a camera along. It was something I never did.

Did you spend time at Graceland?
Yeah, Graceland was great. It was nothing like it is today. I think they've spruced it up a bit now. I've been back there but I didn't go through the house. I waited across the street and I realised that I wanted to remember it the way it was. I remember it really well. I remember his bedroom and I was there several times. When I went there the first time, the guys were teasing me because they said that you could see through my dress! Yeah, I rode fast go-carts out in front yard, I loved riding horses and we went motorcycle riding too. He once took me to all the places around Memphis where he used to live. We went to his high school and the first house that he bought for his mother on Audubon Drive. We went to the movies

too. We did all kinds of fun things.

But Elvis was supposedly happily married to Priscilla at this time.
I always knew that Elvis would never leave Priscilla to be with me. She was away in California or something. Elvis had ways of getting rid of her when he wanted someone else around. I never thought it would be any more that what it was. I never thought he'd leave her and I never thought we'd be together on a regular basis. And I was also still madly in love with James Aubrey anyway.

Is James Aubrey still around?
No, he died when he was seventy-seven or seventy-eight. He died in the early eighties. I saw him here and there but we didn't really stay friends. His daughter is my best friend to date. Once I got past James and started to know him as a person, I really lost respect for him.

Are you married now?
No, I'm not married any longer. I was married to an international lawyer but we got divorced over ten years ago. I'm now single but I do have a boyfriend. Everything is great now.

Glad to hear it. Elvis spoilt just about everyone around him but I know you spoilt him in return. I understand you bought him a ring?
I bought him that ring and it went up for auction recently. I didn't really have a lot of money but I did save up to buy him that from a jeweller in Beverly Hills. It was a big ring and Elvis loved it. He'd like to get his jewellery case and go through various rings telling me about them.

I've got an odd question regarding a habit you supposedly picked up from Elvis. I wondered if you still sleep with cotton in your ears?
I do if I go travelling. You know, it's really weird but Elvis used to wet some cotton, roll it into a little ball then put it into his ear. He could then sleep without being disturbed by loud sounds. Yes, I still do that and I always think of Elvis (laughs).

Finally, what are your thoughts when you look back on what's happened in your life?
I never had any parenting or guidance growing up and I was existing in this fast crazy world. I started as a nobody and I became a young starlet dating these wealthy exciting men... legends. But it's not over yet. There's far more to come!

❝The second chapter of my book was more fun to write than any other... it caused me to think back to the beginning of Presleymania, how it all started, and how exciting those days were.❞

Wink Martindale

Firstly Wink, can I ask how Elvis first came to be on your *Saturday Night Dance Party* in 1956?

I had met Elvis previously at WHBQ that night in 1954 when Sam Phillips brought Dewey Phillips *That's All Right*, the first Elvis record, to play on the air.

We struck up a friendship from that night forward and remained friends until the day he died in the summer of 1977.

As you know, the Colonel didn't want Elvis to appear on any television shows - radio too for that matter - simply because he wanted the Elvis mystique to continue growing. But thanks to the combined friendships of George Klein and Dewey Phillips, Elvis consented to come on to the *Top Ten Dance Party* as a guest that Saturday afternoon in 1956. Also, Gladys and Vernon watched the show on a regular basis so when he was in town he watched as well.

He was well aquainted with the show and its popularity with teens and adults alike. He wanted to promote a charity show for the Cynthia Milk Fund, at which he would be performing at the Overton Park Shell that summer. The day he came on the show he had just returned from Hollywood, from filming the movie *Love Me Tender*.

Do you remember Elvis taking a fancy to Anita Wood on the show?

Oh yes, without a doubt. Anita became my second co-host on the show after the original co-host, Susie Bancroft left to get married. I had known Anita in our mutual hometown of Jackson, Tennessee [eighty-five miles from Memphis] and she was not only very attractive but talented as well.

I recommended her to my bosses as the replacement for Susie and she was an immediate hit.

Naturally, when Elvis watched and saw her, he too was attracted to her. As I recall, he had our mutual friend George Klein call Anita and arrange to have her come to Graceland and, as they say, the rest is history. They dated on and off for quite a lengthy period and from what I understand, they were very much in love back then.

Did you see Elvis on any occasion after he attended *Dance Party* as a guest?

Oh yes, many times. I was never one of the so called Memphis Mafia but we were the kind of friends where if we didn't see each other for months and months, when we finally did see each other, our friendship picked right up where it had left off.

Were you around when Elvis got inducted?

As far as Elvis going into the Army was concerned, like many of us, I simply watched that episode in his life and career from afar.

In California, whose decision was it to start up another *Dance Party* and was it something you wanted to do?

Well actually, I left WHBQ in Memphis for KHJ in Los Angeles at my own

request. I felt I had advanced my career in Memphis just about as far as possible. I went to my mentor and boss who had given me my big shot on television and radio, Bill Grumbles, and asked if he would help me get to either New York or Los Angeles where RKO General owned stations. It turned out to be LA, and I've never been sorry. Once in Los Angeles in March of 1959, I took over the KHJ Radio morning show from 5am to 9am and by that summer, they asked me to duplicate the same successful *Dance Party*-type show I had hosted in Memphis. We even had the same sponsor in both places, Coca-Cola.

How did you get the Colonel to let Elvis do a live transatlantic phone interview with you for the first *Dance Party* show at KHJ?

Simple. As far as I know nobody - including Elvis - asked the Colonel, we just did it. Elvis agreed to help me kick-off my new show and through his people and my people, we set up the time and place for him to be available for the phone conversation. The clarity wasn't all that good, but it was Elvis and that was all that really mattered.

Did you see or talk with Elvis in the sixties when you both lived in LA?

Yes, several times. I must admit, I never tried to be pushy in taking advantage of our friendship. One time, right after he returned from the Army and was filming *GI Blues* at MGM, my *Dance Party* producer Al Burton and I went over to the studio and had some pictures made with Elvis. He was so good about consenting to that sort of thing. My producer had never met Elvis and I still recall how excited he was about that special day. In fact, one of the pictures taken on the set is in my autobiography *Winking At Life* along with a whole series of pictures taken the day Elvis was guest on my *Top Ten Dance Party* in Memphis. The entire second chapter of my book was more fun to write than any other simply because it caused me to think back to the beginning of Presleymania, how it all started, and how exciting those days were.

How did you get the job as narrator for The Elvis Presley Story in 1972?

The producer at Watermark Productions, Ron Jacobs and his partner Tom Rounds, knew of my friendship with Elvis and they wanted someone with a Southern accent to give the show more authenticity. I was pleased, delighted and truly honoured to have been asked to host the show. I was a radio personality at Gene Autry's KMPC in LA when the twelve-hour show was sold to stations on a syndicated basis and part of my hosting arrangement was that I would have the exclusive right to air the show during my noon-3pm time slot on KMPC. The show was heavily promoted on the station and the ratings were terrific - Which was no surprise really.

Did you see Elvis during his final years?

Yes but it was a bittersweet moment for both Sandy and I. As you know, long before I met my wife of twenty-five years, she had dated Elvis on and off for about six years. She had met him at one of her father's nightclubs in Los Angeles and he immediately took a shine to her. But she was too young for him in her mother's eyes and she even went along on many of their early dates. How fun that must have been for everybody involved, huh? Sandy and I were married August 2nd, 1975, and our last visit with Elvis was during one of his concerts in Las Vegas about six months prior to his death. After his performance, Elvis invited Sandy and I backstage to his dressing room where we talked for about half an hour. He had seen us that day as guests on a Bert Convey hosted show on CBS called *Tattletales*. This was a contest between three couples to see which couple knew the most about each other [similar to the British programme *Mr. and Mrs. - Ed*]. Well we won and Elvis was amazed that we knew so much about one another.

At one point Elvis went on and on about how happy he was that my career had gone so well since my days in Memphis. I remember saying to Sandy later, "What's wrong with this picture? Elvis is telling me how well I have done!" It was funny but we enjoyed that visit so much, a visit that would turn out to be our last with him. It was fun seeing him and talking to him, but also sad because his body and his face showed the ravages of time.

As we left the dressing room that night I turned to Sandy and said, "Honey, I'm afraid that's the last time we'll see Elvis alive," and when we arrived back at our hotel room and closed the door behind us, we both broke down and cried. Again, a bittersweet night but one that we shall both cherish in our memories forever.

Did you ever visit Elvis at Graceland?

I didn't and I don't believe Sandy did either. Of course we have been to Graceland on more than one occasion since his death. We had the pleasure of taking part in Elvis Week four years ago, which included a sort of seminar or round table of friends answering fans' questions at Humes High School. This is organised and presented

beautifully each year by Patsy Andersen and it was most enjoyable. We also got to experience the candlelight vigil at Graceland.

What are your views on *Elvis - The Concert*?

I had the honour of co-presenting it along with George Klein, at the initial *Elvis - The Concert* where he sings on stage via past concert videos with his live band and a concert orchestra. That was quite a night too.

Just recently we saw *Elvis - The Concert* again at Universal Amphitheatre here in Los Angeles and it was better than ever. Any Elvis fan who didn't see this virtual concert with the King of Rock 'n' Roll really missed a treat.

Do you know if Elvis' complete *Dance Party* appearance will ever be released on home video or DVD in the future?

That's sadly impossible. Although I still have the audio of that memorable and somewhat historical interview, I made the mistake of loaning my original kinescope (the filmed interview) to friends over the years, and I stupidly failed to make a copy of the master. So the result is that today, I am left with only about three minutes of an almost twenty-five minutes interview. Naturally I should have protected that interview with my life but I failed to do so. Hindsight is always 20-20 isn't it?

It certainly is. Do you have any final thoughts you'd like to share with us Wink?

In closing, I would just like to add that I feel very fortunate to have been a small part of the life of Elvis Presley. I was there at the beginning and I was there at the end. I dwell only on the positive side of his life because there were far more positives than negatives. He gave the world so much happiness during his brief lifetime and that is what I choose to remember.

"That sound was the greatest thing I'd ever heard - even as a kid."

Marsha Alverson

It's difficult not to be envious of Marsha Alverson. After all, Marsha did what millions of other women have only dreamt about. In fact, what many new Elvis fans are too young to even think about! Marsha, now married to well known Elvis photographer Keith Alverson, got her reward for waiting patiently in line, when she took her seat on the front row in Huntsville in 1975.

Polly Hearn caught up with Marsha in Memphis, to share her memories from this show and others when maybe, just maybe, Elvis would notice her...

Marsha, when did you first become an Elvis fan?
Probably when I was about nine years old. *Don't be Cruel* and *All Shook Up* were the first songs I heard on the radio. My dad was stationed in the military, so I was in Bermuda. I had no TV and no radio between 1954 and 1956 and so I did not hear *Heartbreak Hotel* or any of the Sun recordings because I had no access. We got back to the States in '56 and that's when *Don't Be Cruel* and *All Shook Up* were out. That's when I really thought about him.

I thought that sound was the greatest thing I'd ever heard, even as a kid.

Why did Elvis stand out from other artists?
Well, I guess just his voice. It was so dynamic. And then if you put that voice, and even as a youngster you see him. I mean, he was a very nice looking man, even for a kid. Then you just wanted to get more and more of him! When the movies came out, I didn't get to see some of the early ones, as that was when we were out of the

States. But I saw them all from when he came out of the army, you know, from *GI Blues* all the way to the last one. I couldn't wait until a new movie came out.

Did you dream about seeing him in concert?
Yes! But, I never thought I would. It was just too hard to imagine. I never thought I would ever see him. I didn't really know how you'd go about seeing him when he started touring; I had no idea. I didn't know he was in Vegas in 1969. I didn't know until 1971 and that's the first time I was able to get a ticket. I was twenty-three at that time.

When was the first time you saw Elvis on stage?
I saw him in Alabama, the University of Alabama. Everyone you talk to in the South, that was the first place that they saw him. I'm not sure if that is one of the very first places he came, but I've talked to so many people that say November 14th 1971 was the first time they saw him. I just thought it was unbelievable. I didn't have a great seat, it was kind of up and to the side, but when he came out it was just like 'Ohhh, I can't believe I'm here and he's actually on that stage!' It was just so exciting.

Did you buy lots of souvenirs?
Yeah, I bought the poster book, the poster, the programme book, the button and... yeah, lots of things.

How many times did you see Elvis?
Twenty-one times.

Could you pick out a favourite show?

I guess where I had two front row seats; one in 1975, and one in 1976. In 1975 I mailed for tickets, I was very lucky to get a front row seat. And then in 1976, I had to queue in line for two and half days to get my ticket. I had people come up to me and say they would offer me any amount of money if they could have my place in line. I had as much as $1,000 offered for my place. I couldn't give it up.

How much would you have taken?
Oh no. I don't know if I'd have taken anything because it was my second time, that close. I just really don't think any money could have bought it. You would have had the money and then you would have thought, I still wish I had a seat.

Did you spend a long time deciding what to wear?
No, I had gone out and bought something new to wear especially. Both years I had jumpsuits. In the 1970s, I guess jumpsuits were just the style. I had a yellow jumpsuit in 1975 and a red jumpsuit in 1976. I thought you had to get really dressed up because you really thought he might just notice you and you only! When you knew you had a front row seat, you felt like he might get to touch you and you know, get a scarf, or whatever.

There are some pictures where Elvis noticed you and you gave him a gift. Tell me about that.
I had a plaque that year at the Civic Centre, it was the bi-centennial year for the USA, and so everything was red, white and blue. The plaque was like that. It had the Civic Centre sign and it had Elvis' first record, the green and pink letters of his name. I just kind of held it up and I was sitting right in front if him. Finally he said, "Come here," when he got

to that part of the show. You know, he had a certain part of the show where he gave scarves away, like *Love Me Tender* and *Love Me*. Both years I got up on *Love Me* and now of course, that is one of my all time favourite songs.

So Elvis called you up to the stage?
Yeah, the first year in 1975 I had this little button. It had a light on it and lit up when pressed. When it was dark, he saw me flashing it at him. Both years I was so lucky, because when I got up to the stage, there was no rushing. There wasn't a hundred girls all trying to get to the stage. Of course, there was security, but it was just one on one. I didn't have to fight my way or anything.

Were you trembling?
Yeah! He asked what the little light was. He said, "What's this?" You can hear it on one of the tapes of the show, kind of under his breath 'cos he was trying to sing and hold the mike. He could not find the button and so I pressed it and that's when his face lit up. That's how the smile came and thankfully it was captured on film. In fact, when you see the sequenced pictures, I thought my time was over but Elvis was still down, he hadn't got up, and I had sat down. I had turned around and sat down in my seat. Then I saw that he was still down and he was trying to work the button. I saw that he couldn't and so I got back up to help him and so I ended up going twice!

When I sat back down I had the button in my hand. I'm kind of glad I did, because it probably would have got thrown out somewhere and at least he held it in his hand and I got to keep it. When I look at the picture now, I can see that I put my hand on his leg. I didn't even realise at the time.

How did you find the photographs of Elvis and you at this concert?
I found the photographs during an Elvis Week convention years later. This guy just had them out on the table and my

friend called me over. I was very excited when I saw the photographs. You see, on one picture you can see the little guard who let me stand on his chair.

You stood on a chair?
Yeah, the stage was about six-foot high there. It was one of those fold-up chairs and I had really high heels on. I just knew that at any minute the chair was going to fold up with me in it!

Did he kiss you?
Oh yeah. Right on the mouth! There were two that got up before me. An older lady and a younger girl and it was kind of like, when am I going to make my move? I was so nervous. I wasn't used to doing that sort of thing.

What do you remember most about that moment?
I just thought he was so handsome, especially in 1975. He still looked good in 1975.

Is there anyone else that you have since seen in concert that comes close?
Well, I've seen Neil Diamond, but he's not Elvis! I like a lot of the country singers but they don't come close.

Nobody you would queue two days for?
No, Nobody!

And finally, how do you think Elvis should be remembered?
For his music. I think he should be remembered for all the good things he did. All the negative stuff shouldn't be talked about. We can't change anything and why remember the bad things when he did so much good and made so many people happy that I just think that the good times are what everybody should remember.

" Elvis was always on time, he always knew his lines and he never talked back to the director or anything. He was a delight to work with. **"**

Pat Priest

When Pat Priest was a young girl, her family moved from Salt Lake City to Bountiful, Utah. Although her childhood was spent in a small town, she got quite a bit of exposure to entertainment work through her mother.

When Pat reached her junior year in high school, they relocated to Washington, DC and Pat soon started taking the crown in beauty contests. Pat discovered, however, that she had inherited her mother's interest in show business and after an appearance on Art Lamb in Washington, she left the Washington social scene and made her way to California. She got some experience under her belt working in community theatre, including the Alameda Little Theatre, the London Circle Players in Oakland, and the Players of the Golden Hind in Berkeley. This led to a few local TV commercials and she soon began getting guest shots on all kinds of TV shows.

Although not fully retired yet (she

now makes the occasional TV appearances), Pat and her second husband, Fred Hansing, are settled in Haley, Idaho. She makes frequent public appearances at conventions and autograph shows.

Her appearance with Elvis came in 1967 in *Easy Come, Easy Go* where she played Dina Bishop - the bad girl who gets in Elvis' way while he and Dodie Marshall search for treasure.

Andrew Hearn was recently lucky enough to interview Pat about her time spent with Elvis and her memories from that movie...

Tell me a little bit about yourself, you appeared in the TV series *The Munsters* is that correct?
Yes, I did, that show has been on the air continuously for thirty-five years, isn't that hard to believe?

So that show was on in the '60s?
We filmed from '64 to '66.

Now, is it true that you're the daughter of Ivy Baker Priest, the former Treasurer of the United States?
Yeah, yeah, I had a very famous mother in government in the United States and you know, I like to say that it's like water, water everywhere and not a drop to drink. Well, that same thing applied with the money! That's an autograph that I'm collecting.

Of your Mother's?
Right.

Regarding Elvis Presley then, how did you get the roll in the movie *Easy Come, Easy Go?*
Well, they just called me, Hall Wallis, the producer did. I had just finished *The Munsters* and Hall Wallis who was over at Paramount studios, called me for an interview. He talked with me and I, you know.... I didn't really know that much about the movie. He did tell me, I didn't read the script at all, that he'd always had a brunette as the bad girl and a

blonde as the good girl. This time he had decided he was going to have the blonde as the bad girl and the brunette as the good girl. He thought I was very wholesome and American looking so it was literally through this interview.

Okay. Were you excited when you heard that you'd be starring with Elvis Presley?
Oh, very much so, very excited. But, you know, at that time, everything was like a job. We never thought about collecting anything, keeping anything or having anybody's autograph. Over the years I worked in films I never had anybody's autograph, script or anything. I mean, it just never occurred to you so I made a very foolish mistake.

Can you remember your first meeting with the King? What were your first impressions and what was he like to work with?
Okay, my first impressions were not only that but it was how I felt about him all the way through the movie. He was shy, quite shy, he was quite religious and he had his whole entourage of guys who were very, very polite. He was always on time, he always knew his lines and he never talked back to the director or anything. He was a delight to work with and this was all the way through the movie.

Is this all on a professional level?
Well the only way I ever worked with him was on a professional level. Priscilla was very much in the picture at that time although I never did meet her. They weren't married at that time but she was very much in the picture. He was an absolute perfect gentleman.

Do you know if he actually liked the movie?
I think he did yes. I think he liked all the movies he did. They were just typically Elvis. You know, he could just relate to them as his way of life with his singing and all.

No I never did, and that's a regret I have. I really should've got to some of the shows in Vegas; it would've been nice.

So what's your fondest memory of Elvis? What sticks in your mind the most?
I think his gentleness, his politeness, his manners and his way with people.

Good answer. Now, is it true that Elvis hated water? How did he manage in the film?
I didn't know that he hated water and if he did, he never said, however, all of the water scenes were done by stunt men.

When you were working with him, did Elvis mention any plans to do more live appearances?
No he didn't and I don't even know if he did any more movies after that. Andrew, you probably know more about this than I do.

Off the top of my head there was another seven or eight movies after yours. Do people still ask you about your time with Elvis?
Yes, all the time. He still has a fabulous following and when I go to the memorabilia shows I have three photos of me with Elvis and those are amongst my best selling because all the people that collect Elvis memorabilia want it. A lot of people don't even remember and they say "Oh yes, I remember that movie" and so they're forgotten about.

My last question is how do you think the world should remember Elvis Presley?
I think they should remember him as he was in his young years and not as he became. I think that is the way he's remembered, as a kind, wonderful loving person and you know, just respectful. A wonderful singer and the greatest legend of our time, he was one of the great performers.

Did you ever socialise with Elvis and the guys off set when you weren't filming?
I did with the guys. I went out a couple of times with Sonny and Red West and I still keep in touch to this day with Joe Esposito who was his best man.

Did Elvis give you anything as a gift or keepsake?
No, he didn't give me anything but when the movie was over he had a black Eldorado Cadillac convertible with an all black leather interior and he told me he was going to sell it so I asked if I could buy it from him. He did end up selling it to me for $3,000 with the key-chain that said EP on it. But being very foolish I drove it for a couple of years then traded it in for a Pontiac. I didn't trade it as Elvis' car, but just a car.

You mean you just sold it as a normal car?
Just sold it as an automobile. I never told anybody that it was Elvis' car either, even with the keychain. So I threw away my retirement fund!

Yes, I guess you did. Did you ever see or speak to Elvis again after the completion of the film?

Thanks so much for your time Pat, it's been a pleasure talking to you about your time with Elvis.

" Elvis was my hero and I think he should always
be remembered as a symbol of a true
showman, a true entertainer, a true star. "

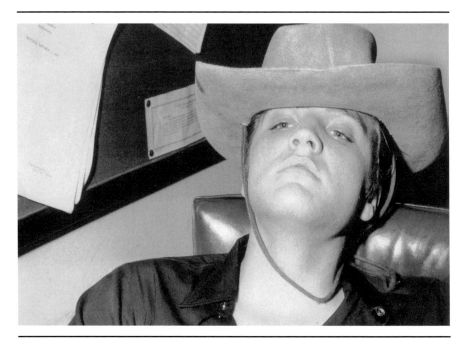

Eamonn Holmes

Millions of homes in the UK wake up each morning to Eamonn Holmes. As a presenter on *GMTV* he is perhaps one of the most familiar and loved faces in the morning - some might say the King of Breakfast TV. Eamonn recently chatted to Polly Hearn about his love for Elvis and why he is such a big fan.

How do you feel about being an Elvis fan?
The thing that annoys me the most is the way you are perceived if you are an

Elvis fan. It's like I've had to come out of the closet over the last couple of years about Elvis. I think I've found the bigger I've got, the more obvious it is, the bigger in size that is! The thing that annoys me most about when you say you're an Elvis fan is people automatically associate you with being slightly freaky or weird. I think it's such a travesty that people can't see beyond a tabloid newspaper image that sells an image of man that gorged himself on fried peanut butter sandwiches and should look at this guy who was so cool and so hip, except for his movies, and was the king of music. I am a genuine

Elvis fan. It was when I was in my late teens and I think the album *Aloha from Hawaii* really got me introduced to Elvis.

You mentioned that you are not a big fan of the movies. Why is that?
No, I think his movies are dire. Yes, you can go through them and cut out the music videos as such. I have to say that I was never an Elvis movie fan. They were so obvious weren't they? He wasn't the worst actor in the world, but he wasn't the best actor in the world. All the movies around at the time were people like Cliff Richard all singing and dancing and I wasn't a big fan of musicals. Although, I remember when I was young in the 1960s, you had to go to the cinema on a Saturday afternoon to give your mum and dad a break. Sometimes we saw Elvis movies. I think maybe I hated them because of that - being forced to go and see them!

Why is Elvis is so special to you?
I like Elvis because he's a man's man and yet a women's man as well. So many stars are exclusive to either women liking them or men liking them, but I think that Elvis is one of those that crossed the divide. You know it's not unmanly to say you like Elvis, where as it is a bit unmanly to say you like Leonardo DiCaprio. When I listen to Elvis music, when I'm alone or when I'm in the car, the music is always catchy and there is always such a range of it. I think it does help that for someone like myself you really quite fancy yourself as Elvis in the shower or the bath!

Not just in the shower eh? You once posed as Elvis on GMTV's charity week *Get Up & Give*.
They forced me into it! I don't think that I do Elvis to a degree that I can go public with it! We had to do these forfeits for charity and everyone in the office, knowing that I am a bit of an Elvis fan, thought I should do Elvis. Then it came closer and closer and I really did worry about it and I chickened

out of it actually. Then I said look, the only way I'll do it is if you get an impersonator on as well. So we got a guy on called Adam. I thought that it would be fine if he sang the song and I just came in with 'I'm all shook up - uh huh huh' and that was it.
It was all very quick because it was at the end of the show. I just turned the collar of my suit up and we had these lovely big '50s microphones. When I was on holiday with the kids this year in America, I went into this shop and they sold these Elvis glasses with sideburns attached to them. I thought this is perfect, so I put them on and it was all already there!

We first bumped into you at *Elvis - The Concert*, what did you think of it?
I honestly thought that it was one of the most exciting nights of my life! I really did. I just thought, what a concert. I was really interested in how it would work, would it work? The hairs on the back of my neck stood up. They really tingled that night. I really thought it worked and it's so clever. To take an original band and backing singers and to project Elvis on to those three different screens at the back. Very, very clever. I honestly think anyone who's been to see it knows, you just let yourself go and you suspend belief for that couple of hours. It was as if you were attending one of his concerts. I really thought it was fantastic. If I had discovered it earlier and if I had been able to follow the tour around the world I definitely would have gone back somewhere. I kept looking at the tour dates thinking, could I get to Paris? Then suddenly it went from Paris to South Africa or something.
I desperately wanted to go to the Memphis one but I was in the middle of recording a game show in Belfast.

Frank Skinner recently said in an article for *Essential Elvis* that he hadn't really enjoyed the concert, because he kept looking at the empty space on the stage

in front of him. Did you feel like that at all?
Everyone goes to concerts and they're usually an anti-climax. Either the sound isn't right or it doesn't sound the way it does on the record, or you've got such a crud seat that you can't see the artist. So therefore a lot of them have back projection these days and I just kept trying to convince myself that he was there. So, it really, really thrilled me. I knew he wasn't going to be there but it was just fantastic. Then I thought, I've never seen Frank Sinatra, I wonder if they could do that for him? You just kept thinking about all the people that they could do this sort of thing for and now when people go on stage are they recorded with that in mind. I mean *Elvis - The Concert* was put together from footage that wasn't originally designed to do that.

Do you think that the concert rediscovered you as an Elvis fan?
I was uplifted by how many different types of people were there. There were people in shirts and ties, yes people in Elvis costumes, but also young people and lots of young girls and blokes. It was great how new generations have discovered Elvis long after he has died. I think the lovely thing we get from *Essential Elvis* is information on new projects and material. If there is new material, something else to talk about, something else to look at, something else to listen to then that's what it's all about. You just wait for the next material from your hero to come out, whether that is Elvis or Kylie Minogue.

Seeing the tribute single today, these tracks are all available but the fact that this is enhanced and it has been released for the American Red Cross Disaster Relief Fund means you want to get hold of it. Anything new that keeps the interest alive is great.

This year has seen a lot of Elvis projects including the release of the all-new *That's The Way It Is* on DVD. What did you think of the film?

I thought it was excellent. I have this indulgence. A DVD projection, which means in an ordinary sized room you can have a cinema screen that is about eight foot by five foot and it just comes down on the wall. The DVD projection makes it just like cinema. I watched *That's The Way It Is* on that. I thought it was superb. I thought there were a lot of good special features and it was really very amusing too. The thing is, again about singing in the shower, singing Elvis songs you tend to impersonate Elvis impersonators impersonating him - if you know what I mean! [Eamonn breaks out into a typically impersonator-style version of *Love Me Tender*]. It's usually a lot deeper in my case, but when you actually listen to Elvis it's quite high pitched. Though he had the ability to change his range whenever he wanted to. My other half, Ruth, wasn't really into Elvis, but when she saw the movie she just kept saying 'he's bloody gorgeous. Look at him - look how gorgeous he is'... you know I used to be gorgeous too! He had it all.

There are so few true world superstars. Lots of people would like to take the crown and I think that a lot of people equate exposure and media coverage with being famous. You really respect someone who has got a true talent and there is nobody who could doubt that Elvis Presley could sing. Nobody could say, that his voice was not up to much. His voice was totally different; his renditions were really quite unique. He also had presence and likeability.

You're working on your own special Elvis project now aren't you?
As well as hosting *GMTV*, I also present *Songs of Praise* for the BBC. I put a project to them, where I said I think we should do a *Songs of Praise* on Elvis Presley. It was immediately dismissed and people asked why should we? I said, because, and I think I'm right in saying, that he was the biggest selling gospel recording artist ever. Then I started showing these people songs, like *How Great Thou Art*. We could interlink the

programme with tributes from recording artists of today singing, like Sting or Bono through to archive footage of Elvis. Particularly looking at the influence of the black gospel groups and the effect that they had on Elvis' music. I'm very, very hopeful that with a bit of support to BBC *Songs of Praise* that this project will be realised next year for the anniversary and we will get an *Elvis Tribute Songs of Praise* special coming from Graceland or somewhere. I really hope that the programme will come off and what I'm hoping to do is start a bit of interest off now. It would be great if people would start writing to you, or me, with their ideas or thoughts and support for the programme.

What are you recollections of the day Elvis died?

In 1977, I was working in a club behind the bar and I remember it was a Wednesday night. These guys came in and said, "Did you hear the news? Did you hear about Elvis?" I was like, what? Then when they said that he had died, I was like... well, I never served another drink all night. There was a hush and people left. Out the back there was a radio in the storeroom and we tuned into Radio Luxembourg when the tribute programmes began. I remember that we shut the bar early, everyone had gone to hear the news. It's not like today where you have Sky News or News 24, just one news bulletin in the evening and if you missed it, then that was it. There must have been specials because radio was getting much more reactive than television of course.

I remember in the taxi on the way home listening to his music and then when I got home, putting on Radio Luxembourg and listening to someone like Paul Gambaccini, in fact I'm sure it was Paul Gambaccini. Listening to way into the early hours of the morning to share in people's grief from the phone-ins and that. It was a grief too. It was on a par with 'Who shot Kennedy?'

And finally, how do you think that Elvis should be remembered?

I remember really getting into Elvis the last two years before he died but I suppose when you look at him in the 1968 comeback and the *That's The Way It Is* era, then that is the best physical image you're going to get. I really liked that album *Moody Blue* and thought there was some good stuff on that. I think everyone needs a hero. That's my view. I think your life must be pretty dull if you don't have a hero. However real that hero is there is also an element of fiction and that's why in my line of business it's better not meeting some people because you can shatter illusions. Elvis was a hero - one of a small band of heroes for me in life and I think he should always be remembered as a symbol of a true showman, a true entertainer, a true star. Elvis should be remembered as someone who could unite fellas and girls, and not somebody to be laughed and mocked at. If you look at today's stars there is nobody, and has been nobody since Elvis Presley. In his small finger he had more talent than most of them will ever have in their lives so, he should be remembered simply as 'The man!'

> **"** I treasure the fact that I was able to be a part of Elvis' life and witness first-hand the entertaining, sensitive and loving man that he was. **"**

Ginger Alden and Rosemary Alden

In her first fan-based magazine interview, the local beauty who became Elvis' fiancée, talks exclusively to Andrew Hearn about her amazing relationship with the King.

Ginger Alden, along with her sister Rosemary, finally break their silence about life with Elvis...

Can I start by asking you both to describe the circumstances leading up to your initial visit to Graceland and meeting Elvis for the first time?
Ginger: I first met Elvis when I was five-years-old. I know my sister Rosemary is telling about this first meeting so I will jump to the evening of November 19th 1976. George Klein called my sister

Terry, the reigning Miss Tennessee, asking if she would like to meet Elvis. My sister was engaged at the time but thought, of course it would be nice to see Graceland and to meet Elvis. She told George yes, but felt awkward going alone. My sister Rosemary suggested that she and I accompany Terry saying they could always ask us to leave.

We arrived at Graceland and were escorted upstairs and into his daughter Lisa's bedroom. I know this sounds funny, but when Elvis entered the room, I thought trumpets would sound. He looked so handsome. He quickly sat in a chair and started talking with each of us. It turned out to be a truly wonderful evening as he took us on a tour of Graceland. Later he sang for us and read aloud from some of his books about religion.

Rosemary: We had initially first met Elvis quite a few years earlier when our father was a Public Relations Officer in the army in Memphis. (We even have several photos of our father with Elvis just after he was inducted).

When Elvis returned from Germany and was no longer in the service, our family was invited, by an uncle of Elvis', to join him and a group at the local fairground. I was twelve at the time and Ginger was five. Elvis remembered my father and walked over to meet him and our family. He was so kind and cordial. He shook hands with each of us and patted Ginger on the head. We never dreamed our paths would cross again or that in fifteen years time, Ginger would become engaged to Elvis!

Ginger, within just days of meeting you, Elvis' seemed to be in constant high spirits, especially on stage. One of his best live shows was the New Year's Eve show on December 31st 1976 in Pittsburgh. Can you describe your recollections of that evening?
I went to almost every one of Elvis' shows after meeting him and I felt his voice was in the best shape during the

last years of his life. It was always great to see him performing at his best and having a great time as with the New Year's Eve show. Like any performance, some shows are just better than others be it sound problems or just being tired. I know Elvis always tried to give 100% for his fans.

He was always so happy when Lisa was able to be at his shows. I always sat in a chair near the stage and during that particular show, I remember holding Lisa up so she could have a better view of his performance.

Are there any specific shows that stand out in your mind Rosemary?
There were several shows. The first one being the Las Vegas shows that Elvis had our entire family flown in to see. We were flown in on his private jet called The Jetstar. What fantastic performances Elvis gave! Ginger had already been in Vegas with Elvis while he was performing two shows a night for two weeks.

There was also a great show in which Elvis called my sister Terry onstage to play a classical piece.

I can't remember exactly which city we were in but during one show, I needed to go to the ladies room and asked Ginger if she would go with me. She said okay but we would have to hurry back before Elvis started his introduction of his band because he usually would introduce Ginger and our family as well.

As we were returning, the stage door jammed and we could not get back... all I could think was, what is Elvis going to think when he starts to introduce us and we aren't there? We finally got the door open and just in time for Elvis' introduction! Later that evening, I told Elvis what happened and he thought it was so funny! While performing the very next night, he jokingly said, "Rosemary, you just stay put!" He was so very funny. We loved his sense of humour as it reminded us so much of our own.

I was so happy as he presented a green velvet box, opened it and placed a very large and beautiful diamond ring on my finger. My hand was shaking as we kissed and stepped out of the bathroom into his bedroom. My hand was still trembling as he kept lifting it to look at the ring saying, "oh, boy." We were congratulated by his stepbrothers and Charlie Hodge gave us a small backgammon game as a quick gift.

Rosemary: I know we were all so happy for them both after Ginger came home and showed us her beautiful 11fi carat diamond engagement ring which we later found out had been especially made from his TCB ring that he always wore on stage. I remember thinking now Elvis won't be alone anymore and will have a family again.

Do you still have your engagement ring Ginger?
Yes I do.

Elvis proposed on January 26th 1977 at Graceland. Can you give us your recollections and reactions to what happened that day?
Ginger: When January 26th came, I felt as if I had known Elvis longer than a few months. Our relationship had been so intense as if he wanted me to know almost everything about him in a short time. I knew I had fallen in love and couldn't imagine not being with him.

His cousin Billy had told me how Elvis would come in from riding motorcycles, fall across the bed and say, "There must be someone out there for me." We had been together a short time but I felt I had found my soul mate. There was a lot of activity going on that day at Graceland and it had to do with me getting my engagement ring. I was called into his bathroom where Elvis then said many beautiful things ending his proposal with, "I never thought that I would find it in my own backyard, I'm asking you, will you marry me?"

Can you tell us more about the trip to Hawaii in March 1977? The photographs from the time indicate that Elvis was in excellent spirits (playing football, relaxing on the beach and generally having fun). You were all there weren't you?
Ginger: My time with Elvis was so special and the Hawaiian vacation was a lot of fun. Elvis knew I had never been to Hawaii and wanted to take my whole family but only my sisters could go at this time.

We left on my sister Terry's birthday, which was March 3rd. He was in a great mood, despite the fact, he had mentioned that more of his group had asked to go along and he reluctantly let them. My sisters and I stayed with Elvis in the back of the Lisa Marie during the flight as he joked, laughed and sang. The trip was so beautiful, but unfortunately cut short when Elvis irritated one of his eyes and we had to return to Memphis. I stayed at Graceland and administered eye cream for a few days so I could help him be prepared for his next tour. I felt he genuinely had a good time on this trip and it was so wonderful to see him relax, go out to a shopping mall and sing. I have never forgotten the thrill of that vacation!

Rosemary: Yes, Elvis wanted to take our whole family but they couldn't leave their jobs so Terry and myself went along with Ginger. We had a great time in Hawaii seeing Elvis relax and take in some sun.

Rosemary, can you tell us about the famous photograph where Elvis is on top of you?
Yes, I have taken a lot of ribbing over the years with that photo! We were at a vacation home in Hawaii and a few of us were talking with Elvis. I noticed that he kept cutting his eyes over in my direction when he suddenly got up, started to walk past me then he threw himself on top of me! Elvis and I were laughing so hard and I just more or less spontaneously, threw my leg into the air and someone took the photo. I still can't help but laugh every time I see that picture!

Apart from the vacation in Hawaii, can you tell us about any other trips that took place with Elvis? We're aware of your Grandfather's funeral, which took place in January 1977.
Ginger: When my grandfather passed away, Elvis was very concerned and really wonderful.

Of course, I wanted to be at my grandfather's funeral and yet I did not want to leave Elvis. He was so sweet in asking if he could accompany me to the funeral and I answered yes. He had my family flown in to Harrison, Arkansas where we drove twenty miles to Jasper, Arkansas for the services, which took place in a very small church. We left Jasper and flew back to Memphis. There was no family get together after the services.

Rosemary: Elvis spent the night at our home one evening. This was something that he told us he never did in his later years. Elvis decided to spend the night after driving Ginger and me home from Graceland.

Early in their relationship, Elvis had asked Ginger to move in to Graceland which she declined explaining that it wasn't her way nor my parents, and Elvis said that he respected her and my parents for that. Elvis also told Ginger that his mother would have loved her morals and values.

We really enjoyed having Elvis as a houseguest. He was always so much fun to be around. I know that Elvis planned on coming to England sometime after he and Ginger were married. He wanted to tour Europe, as he knew his fans had never seen him perform live there. He always had his fans close at heart.

Ginger, what are your recollections of the June 1977 event in Madison, Wisconsin when Elvis got out of the limo you were in to break up a situation at a gas station? Apparently, he spotted two youths ganging up on an attendant.
Elvis always seemed ready to help someone out and noticing a disturbance at a gas station, he quickly got out, approached the youths and left them all shaking hands. He returned to the car as if it was no big deal, but for those of us who witnessed it, it was another moment of seeing Elvis' concern for the welfare of others.

What were some of the topics that you remember Elvis discussing in your presence, either at Graceland or elsewhere? Did he talk about his past, his mother, growing up in Memphis or Tupelo?
Ginger: Elvis loved his parents and spoke with me about his mother on different occasions. I know he really missed her a great deal. He wanted to show me where he was born and different places in his past so we often went out on his

" *I don't see how this writer can live with himself knowing the lies and vicious rumours he has tried to spread about so many as a last ditch sensationalistic grasp at making money off of his association with Elvis.* "

motorcycle around the city and toward Tupelo.

Rosemary: I remember Elvis saying how upset he was with a lot of the people he had working for him. He had already gotten rid of a few. He said that he had several in mind who were on their way out and they were definitely aware of it!

Elvis often spent several days at a time, secluded in his bedroom. Did he ever explain to you why he did that?
Ginger: Elvis had asked me to move into Graceland which I declined explaining that it just wasn't my or my family's way. He told me he understood and respected me for that. When I did visit Graceland, we indeed stayed upstairs quite a bit. I attribute it to the fact that there always seemed to be a flurry of activity going on downstairs. He would often ask me who was downstairs, which was usually an employee with a date or friends and he would say that he didn't want to go down then. After a tour, if he was in his pyjamas or unshaven, he didn't feel comfortable going downstairs where someone could be hanging out that he didn't know.

Rosemary: Elvis loved his privacy. From what I heard, Elvis did not always go downstairs because he never really knew who or what was down there. Elvis stated that he never knew who would be the next in line to pester or hint for something, which made him sick.

Was it apparent to you, at the time, that Elvis may've had a problem with prescription medication?
Was it ever discussed amongst yourselves and in your family?
Ginger: Sorry, I'll have to pass at this time.
Rosemary: I would also rather not discuss this at this time.

Did Elvis ever discuss with you the soon to be released book by Red, Sonny and Dave Hebler, *Elvis: What Happened?*
Ginger: I have been amazed and saddened over the years by the numerous articles and books written by some who turned not only on him but themselves as well. So many untruths! I never knew of Elvis reading a pre-publication transcript of *Elvis, What Happened?* but someone in his group did inform him of it. He was hurt and angry that they had turned and done something like that after he had paid for so much with them and put their kids through school.

Rosemary: I remember that Elvis was extremely upset that the book was being released and that the authors would do something like that to him as he said that he had done so much for them and their families in the past.

There have been some horrific stories that the National Enquirer was called prior to the alarm being raised when Elvis was found in his bathroom on August 16th 1977.
It's a tough question, but would either of you like to throw some light on this allegation?

Ginger: Yes, It is long past time to shine

the light of truth on what is a malevolent fabrication. I don't see how the writer can live with himself knowing the lies and vicious rumours he has tried to spread about so many as a last ditch sensationalistic grasp at making money off of his association with Elvis. There was no phone call made by my mother or myself to anyone dealing with a publication of any type on the day that Elvis died. I was stunned and heartbroken and am appalled that anyone would think differently.

The day after Elvis' death our home was besieged by reporters from all branches of the media and tabloids, all trying to cover this tragedy. You can imagine the scene with more than 500,000 mourners and press from all over the world converging on Memphis. My mother turned everyone away at that time protecting me as I told her I did not want to give any interviews. I finally decided to grant an interview with our local paper to try and set the record straight after seeing Elvis' road manager on our television stating he had found Elvis' body. The tabloids had also returned to our doorstep literally shouting at one another. Next, the National Enquirer told us that Elvis' ex-girlfriend had given them a story and they were going to print a story about his death anyway so that is how my interview in the National Enquirer came about. As distraught as I was at that time and not knowing what in the world would be said about Elvis, I consented to do an interview for the National Enquirer. I remember Elvis telling me when we first started dating that there would be a lot of people who would be jealous of our relationship. He also asked me if I could handle it. I naively answered yes. I never foresaw the kind of self-promoting denigration of his character and memory that has appeared in print and on television since his death.

Rosemary: No, it really isn't a tough question to answer, simply because it did not happen. I hesitate to give any merit by even discussing this ludicrous and sick fabrication, but, for the sake of some of the fans, who have heard of this, and actually spent their money on this person's book (for which they should definitely get a refund. Good luck trying to get it). Here is the truth and nothing but the truth as I (we) would definitely like to clear this up once and for all.

A very jealous employee of Elvis' started this whole sick and malicious tale after he was fired by Vernon Presley after suspecting him of taking photos, selling them to tabloids and even stealing some of Elvis' items to sell. Out of work and with no income, he decided to try and make some money by writing a very malicious fictitious mystery that years later, he had to publish himself as no reputable publisher would dare touch it.

We heard of this through someone who had seen a copy of his manuscript at the courthouse, and wanted us to know. We retained a lawyer and the author of this very sick fabrication seemed to have gotten scared and went back to California. His own lawyer could not even locate him. Years later, he decided to try and pull his little story off. We were taken by surprise. This individual definitely lost his meal ticket when Elvis died. He has been so jealous and harboured such ill feelings toward Ginger and our family because Elvis was planning on him being one of the very next ones to go. He was going to be replaced by my brother Mike. Elvis didn't trust this person after he made some improper gestures toward Ginger just before what would have been Elvis' last tour. Ginger told Elvis about this and he was certainly not happy. This person has also lied about his various places of employment and titles, and even his own military record. Talk about an ego. What some people will do for a buck. This person had absolutely no basis for his book whatsoever.

On the day that Elvis died, neither Ginger nor my mother, spoke with anyone from the National Enquirer or any other publication. Had this happened, the police, Vernon Presley and the news would have all been investigating it. Even all of the tabloids would have had a very big story to tell, but nothing happened. Why? Because it simply did not take place.

Also to clear up another vicious rumour, Ginger rarely took her eye makeup off around Elvis, as he loved her dark eyes. This is why she still had some on the morning that he passed away. It is absolutely unbelievable what vicious lies are out there once you get in the public eye. Ginger had just found the person she deeply loved, dead on the bathroom floor. Her shock and grief were profound and real and for anyone to suggest otherwise is simply not true and sick. If Elvis were alive today, he would certainly be the first to tell you.

I would also like to add that after Elvis and Ginger became engaged, we noticed a drastic change with some of his employees. We knew Elvis was planning on making some changes, or I should say cleaning house, and they knew also. The jealousy at times seemed so thick you could cut it with a knife. It was so overwhelming at times I (we) have often asked the question, what really happened to Elvis or rather could have happened?

What are the true facts behind your mother pursuing the Presley Estate for a swimming pool after Elvis died?
Ginger: Here are the facts concerning my mother's lawsuit: Elvis had been telling me that he would like my family to be closer to Graceland and not have very far to drive. Elvis cared dearly for both of my parents but knew they had had marital problems in the past. He even spoke to both of them about their troubles but a separation and divorce seemed to be the only answer at that time.

When Elvis very generously offered to buy a new home for my mother, he acted as if it was nothing out of the

ordinary for him to do this. While we were on tour, he would often bring up the subject of house hunting and would ask me if my mother had been looking at new homes. I would reply "No", because I knew she didn't feel comfortable going alone and since his gift was so generous, she didn't know what type of homes to even look at.

Elvis wanted to do this and was so excited that he even had his own appointments set up to look at some homes so he could move forward with his plan. We accompanied him on these trips but he wasn't happy with the homes we saw, as he would constantly say there was no room for a pool or the home needed a pool. I finally spoke with my mother and realized she was content in the home we had already been living in. I mentioned this to Elvis and he immediately got on the phone telling her that he wanted to pay for her home and that she should not have the worry of a house-note hanging over her head in her later years. He was genuinely excited as he asked her to bring her payment book and any relevant papers to Graceland and turn everything over to his father Vernon, who would take care everything for him.

The next day my mother arrived at Graceland, graciously thanking Elvis and giving all the necessary papers to his father. Vernon in turn told her that he was turning everything over to their attorney who would handle it. At that time, Elvis even went a step further and informed my mother that not only would he like to pay for her home but he would also like to have some landscaping put in and a swimming pool installed. Once again my mother told Elvis how deeply she appreciated his wonderful gifts. Elvis proceeded with his plans. Two large trees were placed in our front yard and a contract was drawn up to install a swimming pool. Elvis came out to our home, in great spirits, on August the 6th 1977. He viewed the trees in the front yard and once again told us that all we needed

was the pool. Ten days later, Elvis passed away and my mother quit her job to be at home with me through this very sad and difficult time. The swimming pool was also installed shortly thereafter.

My Mother soon received a letter from her mortgage company stating she was three months behind in her house payments. Needless to say, we were absolutely shocked.

I told my mother to call the attorney for the estate, who had all the paperwork, which she did. The attorney sent a letter to my mother, which she still has, that states clearly, and I quote:

'Were Elvis alive there would be no problem in proceeding with the gift he intended to make to you of the payment of the balance owed on your residence. However, the only instrument, which gives Mr. Presley the authority to act is Elvis' will. Because there was no executed contract, Vernon Presley has no authority to complete the gift that Elvis intended to make, and he is without authority under the will or the Statute of Tennessee in order to do this.'

It was obvious to us that the estate was trying to stop all cash outflow after Elvis' death. Shocked and realizing she had quit her job, my mother felt that she had no choice but to file a lawsuit against the estate to insure that Elvis' known promises and intentions were fulfilled. Elvis had thought all of this had been taken care of. We later found out that the parents of Elvis' ex-girlfriend had also been asked to leave the home in which they resided but the estate still owned.

When the case went to the Shelby County Chancery Court, we lost due to the fact that there was no written contract on Elvis' wishes only a verbal agreement. Our attorney took the case to the Tennessee Court of Appeals where they reversed the Chancery courts decision unanimously and the estate was ordered to proceed with Elvis' wishes and pay the mortgage on our

home. The estate had a lot of other lawsuits at the time and took the case to the Supreme Court. We lost once again due to the fact that it was just a verbal agreement.

Rosemary: The truth regarding our mother's lawsuit had nothing to do with the swimming pool. The truth of the matter is that Elvis wanted to move our family closer to Graceland and therefore, wanted to purchase a home for us. Elvis was known for purchasing homes and cars for literal strangers so his gesture and wish was nothing out of the ordinary, especially for his fiancée's family. After Elvis' death, his wishes were not being honoured by his estate, which brought on undue hardships for my mother as she had quit her job and had depended on Elvis' verbal wishes and gesture. Elvis would have wanted our mother to take action, as this is something he definitely wanted done. Elvis even went to his grave thinking that it had been done.

Due to a letter that we obtained, our mother won unanimously in The Court of Appeals. Unfortunately, over the years, the fans did not know the facts regarding this case.

By not knowing or understanding left ill feelings thus, very vicious stories and lies have been circulating for years regarding this matter. We knew that the fans would not understand this lawsuit when it was filed but again, it was something that Elvis would have wanted us to do. Simply put, it was merely honouring Elvis' wishes.

Now that the uncomfortable but necessary questions are out of the way, can I now ask each of you some lighter questions? What's your most treasured moment with Elvis? Maybe there is something special that he may've said or done?
Ginger: The moment Elvis slipped my engagement ring on my finger holds a special place in my heart. I also

treasure the fact that I was able to be a part of his life and witness first hand the entertaining, sensitive and loving man that he was.

When Elvis and I discussed our wedding plans and set our wedding date of December 25th 1977, I remember thinking how appropriate we were back in Lisa's room where I had met him. It was very early morning August 16th and I have always felt that was God's way of letting me know, once again, how Elvis truly felt before God took him and for that I am forever grateful.

Rosemary: My most treasured moment with Elvis occurred when he told our family that he was going to marry Ginger, how happy she made him and how much he loved us as a family while he placed our TLC necklaces around each of our necks. I remember Elvis saying how happy he was. I have always treasured those moments in my heart.

Elvis was obviously a huge part of your life, then and now, can I ask how you think the world should remember him and the legacy he left behind?
Ginger: I think Elvis should be remembered with great respect for his compassion and originality in the music field. His ability to just be himself on film seemed to come without effort for someone who once told me that as an actor the most difficult part was being natural on camera. He was a person looking forward to many changes in his life, who loved and appreciated his fans and would want to be remembered for bringing a smile to their faces and enjoyment into their lives.

Rosemary, we've asked Ginger, and now we'd like to ask you. How do you think Elvis Presley should be remembered by the fans all over the world?
Elvis should be remembered as the truly beautiful person that he was in his kindness and loving ways. His inner soul touched our hearts. He should also be remembered as being the greatest entertainer of our time. Elvis was truly one of a kind and he loved his fans very much.

Thank you both for allowing *Essential Elvis* the opportunity to give its readers a rare insight into the last few months of Elvis' life. It's been a pleasure getting to know the Alden family and we look forward to a long and interesting friendship.

" Elvis and I had a lot of chemistry on screen. There's something magical about that picture. The other beach movies try too hard. "

Joan Blackman

Joan Blackman's first movie was *Good Day For a Hanging* (1958), a typical western with Fred MacMurray. In the next few years she appeared in the Dean Martin film, *Career,* a Tony Curtis comedy *The Great Impostor* and *Visit to a Small Planet*, which gave her a chance to get goofy with Jerry Lewis.

She first met Elvis on the set of *Loving you* and started an on-and-off romance lasting until he sailed to Germany during his national service in the US Army.

Joan played opposite Elvis in one of his most successful films, *Blue Hawaii.* Not only did the film set the formula for many of Elvis' flicks, but it probably got the whole beach movie thing started. Joan played Maile Duvall, whose dark good looks (half Hawaiian and half French according to the script) provided some competition for the Hawaiian scenery. Joan joined forces with Elvis again a year later in *Kid Galahad*, a remake of a Humphrey Bogart classic. She turns up as the sister of Elvis' boss [played by Gig Young], who disapproves of his interest in her.

Joan is a very private person who has always turned down interview requests... until now!

Could we start by asking you for a little information on your background?

Well, I started in show business when I was five years old, I played a doll in *Alice in Wonderland*. From there I went to dancing school. Both my mother and father were very music. They both sang and there was always music at the parties they had, so I grew up around it. I probably knew just about every American standard by the time I was eleven years old without even knowing that I did. So, I starting singing at about the time when the Korean War was upon us, so I used to go to some famous places here in California and entertain the troops. This was before they went off to Korea. Anyway, I was really good at singing. My father started playing bass at around the same time so we joined up with a friend of his who played guitar and went straight out on the road.

It was off to Hollywood at an early age I take it? What did all your friends think about that?

Before I got to Hollywood my mother put me in beauty contests that made everyone hate me. But I finally got there and my picture landed in someone's office and from then on, my success, which happened within three months of being there, was because of the way I looked. Nothing to do with my singing talent or my dancing lessons (laughs). But I did have talent. I didn't know it then but I had something churning around me that someone saw.

Would you say that your interest then was more singing than acting?

Absolutely, always has been. I went to Hollywood to sing and dance in the movies, I didn't really go there to act. Gene Kelly was my hero and I grew up with all those musicals.

So it was musical-type songs that you were singing back then?

Well, first of all, I was only eleven when I first started so when I was fourteen, and started working with bands, people thought I was a lot older. I sang what is now classed as jazz because of all the jazz players that now do the songs that I used to sing. Now they classify standard musical songs as jazz.

Did you have any kind of interest in Elvis at this time? Were you a fan of his?

I had seen Elvis once, on *The Ed Sullivan Show*. Our firm went to Los Angeles and we got there at about the same time. But no, I really wasn't a fan of his at that time.

He didn't make any kind of impression on you at all?

Well, I thought he was cute but I didn't think of him beyond that television show. I didn't faint, scream or do any of those things. I was rather a serious young woman and I was working at a very young age.

So, you met Elvis there in Hollywood?

I met him at Paramount Studios. He was doing *Loving You* and he just saw me and just said "Hey you!" whilst I was just having some lunch one day. I was a little shy, not just of him, but of everything.

Did you date Elvis before *Blue Hawaii*?

Yes, I dated Elvis before he went to Germany. It was on and off for about a year because he'd come here to do what he had to do. He'd take care of business and then go back home again. But he really liked me. He was under contract to Hal Wallis when he went off to Germany. I was under contract to Burt Lancaster, I had a contract with him within a few months of getting to Hollywood.

And after Elvis went to Germany?

After he went to Germany I made my first film and then I went under contract to Hal Wallis myself. Whilst I was there I made two films, which were *Visit to a Small Planet* [a very funny film with Jerry Lewis] and *Career* [with Jerry's partner Dean Martin]. Hal Wallis let me go and Elvis came back. Juliette Prowse was actually set to do *Blue Hawaii*.

Yes, I understand her demands were far too high to be met.
She was also going with Frank [Sinatra] at the time so he influenced her there too. She was French and a gorgeous dancer so I guess they wanted to use her because of that. I really don't know how they came to their conclusion but she was gone and they asked me. Hal Wallis, who I was no longer under contract with, had to get me back at a different price. So, I was signed and did *Blue Hawaii*.

Would you say that *Blue Hawaii* was the movie that really started off the beach films in the 1960s?
Well, yes, I think so. But I also think that none of the others came up to *Blue Hawaii*. I've always thought that there was something very sweet about it, although it now seems a little sentimental. Elvis and I used to look at each other and wonder if they really wanted us to say such dialogue but we had a lot of chemistry on screen. There's something magical about that picture. The other beach movies try too hard.

You sound pretty proud of the movie.
I didn't do any great acting in that film but there's some connection that it has with people. Elvis obviously had a lot to do with that but there was something between us too and that gave it a flavour above any of the others. The other beach movies were kind of just people jumping around in the sand.

Would you say that it was your best movie?
No, oh no. I think my best movie was *Career*. I mean, that's where I really got to act.

But *Blue Hawaii* was your most successful, box office wise?

Sure, it was the most successful but when fans talk to me about the movies I did with Elvis they always seem to like *Kid Galahad*. You know, I never knew if Elvis asked for me for that second picture.

I prefer it to *Blue Hawaii*; in fact I'm actually watching *Kid Galahad* with no sound as I'm talking to you.
Really, what scene is it?

Charles Bronson has just had his fingers broken and he's now trying to do up Elvis' boxing gloves.
Poor old Charlie! (laughs).

How did they get on?
Charlie tried to help Elvis with the boxing thing and I really do believe that Elvis was a little resentful of that, although Elvis was always pretty open to any kind of help given to him. They got along okay but they weren't buddies and they were never going to be either. He didn't exactly come over for dinner, you know? (laughs).

Did he hang out with you and Elvis during breaks and stuff?
No, he didn't. I really don't know how they got along privately. You see, Charlie was a friend of mine long before we did *Kid Galahad* and he isn't the kind of guy who hangs out with a lot of people anyway. He was a very private person and very close mouthed.

What was Elvis' overall attitude towards making those movies?
Actors today kinda take over the movie, and they run the show. Along with the director, the stars have a lot of say. If Elvis was ever uncomfortable with anything or he didn't like someone you wouldn't hear it very loudly. He would simply go off to the side. In both of the movies that I did with him he pretty much did what was wanted of him. Like dialogue, he'd change a word or two but he usually stuck to the script. Even though he was the King, it seemed to me

> **"**I felt sorry for Elvis when I saw him in Vegas, I felt like something had been taken away.**"**

that he accepted word from people who thought it was the right thing for him.

He had a lot of trust in directors didn't he?
Yes but that's too bad. He shouldn't of had because if he'd have gone along with some of his own instincts, he might've done some different kind of films.

Were you supposed to sing in Blue Hawaii?
Yes, I thought I was going to and that was the shame of it. With all my years of singing and dancing they didn't let me. They didn't want to let me share that, it was Elvis that was going to do all singing.

That sounds like the Colonel.
Both Colonel Parker and Hal Wallis made the decision. I just didn't have a chance. They took out any voice I had in the film from the album, apart from the very end when you can hear my voice. I've always wondered about that, as I never got royalties from it.

You're talking about the Hawaiian Wedding Song right?
Yes, that's right.

But you never went into the studio to record anything for the movie?
No, I never recorded anything in the studio.

Did you get to sing with Elvis off set?
Yes, he liked my singing a lot. He looked around like a proud father when I sang.

When we were in Hawaii, after work we'd go outside and he'd bring his guitar and we'd sing together. You know, Elvis could've done that for me, got me a part singing in the film, but there are reasons as to why he didn't and I'll get into those in my book.

Do you remember the titles of any of the songs that you used to sing off set?
I'm trying to think of the one that we did that night Patti Page was there... er ... You know, there are so many things that I can clearly picture, but I don't know why I don't remember. Oh yes, I do know why, it was because there was some emotional tie to it and there was something that happened that threw me. I can't for the life of me remember the first time I saw Elvis after we did *Blue Hawaii*. It was in Hawaii, but I just can't remember the incident.

Do you remember any joking around off set?
Yes, that was really his saving. Unlike all the stories that you hear on television today where people are saying that they were family and that they got along so great, the producer was great, the director was great, we loved each other and had such a good time, our sets were always very hush. This is because the producer wanted it that way and it had a lot to do with Hal Wallis. He was not the kind of person that you had a good time with. Our sets were very serious. So, one of the things that Elvis' guys helped with was the goofing around, the joking, because it eased the tension. Elvis loved it. One of the favourite in-jokes was that if anything wrong happened, like you heard someone talk during a take or something, Elvis would cover his mouth with his hand, imitate a loud speaker. He'd announce that flight so and so (he'd make up a number) was leaving from Hawaii to Memphis (laughs). He needed to do stuff like that because he was not at ease in front of the camera.

Really? That surprises me a little.

Yes, not just because they were formula movies he was churning out, but in certain dialogue scenes he was very nervous. He used to hold my hand until I thought he'd never let me go.

I'm at the end of the movie now. We've just seen the winning fight and you're kissing whilst everyone is leaving the room.
Okay, here's a little kissing story that isn't really going to be telling very much; we had our suites in a hotel in Honolulu and girls would be climbing the fire escapes to get to Elvis. They had a guard at the elevator door so nobody could get onto his floor. Well, I got into the elevator and somehow, these four girls dressed in schoolgirl uniforms got in there and as soon as the doors closed, they just pinned me to the wall. They were hysterical and crying. "Oh, you've kissed him, you've touched him!" they said. I was more in awe of them than they were of Elvis you know? I was speechless. When we got to the top floor, I got out but they weren't allowed to.

So, what about those kisses?
We had a few, but that's all I'm willing to say (laughs).

Okay, on to some less romantic topics; do you recall any of the guys, the Memphis Mafia?
I think the person that I liked the best and was really able to talk with was Sonny West. I loved Sonny because he was the most communicative with me as all of the other guys just talked over my head. They would not talk to me at all and it was almost as if I wasn't there. I don't know if they were told to behave that way, or they just thought that it was expected of them. I did talk to Joe Esposito the other day because he's done a documentary and he wanted me to be in it. I really didn't want to do it and so I pulled out.

Did you ever see Elvis on stage?
I actually sat in the front row with Hal

Wallis during the Pearl Harbour show in 1961, which I couldn't hear. I finally left after just half an hour because the girls just never stopped screaming, not for one minute.

Did you catch any shows in Vegas during the 1970s?
I did, in fact the last time I saw him was in Vegas, when I went with a girlfriend of mine to see his show. He had been doing Vegas for quite a few years and I just figured that it was time for me to see him again. I'd been hearing things and I just wanted to see if there was some kind of connection that I could make.

What year was this? Can you remember?
Let's see. It wasn't long before he died. This had to be around two or three years before that.

And how had he changed?
I was just so taken back. I mean, I had changed too but when I first saw him I was just stunned. It wasn't just the weight but I saw something that made me very sad.

How was the show itself? Was it one of those electric shows or a poor one?
It was okay. I much preferred the stuff he did at the beginning, when he did *Hound Dog* with just the guitar and bass and a few backing singers, it was very soulful. I felt sorry for him when I saw him in Vegas, I felt like something had been taken away.

Did you actually get to speak to him on that final occasion?
I called back stage and I got Joe who said that he knew Elvis would be so happy to see me so I went with my girlfriend and it was a very meaningful meeting. I wanted to reach out to him so badly but I don't think anyone could've at that point. That was the last time I saw him. Maybe if someone had been forceful with him, told him to take a

change, go out on a limb and do that thing you wanted to do when you were just a young actor just starting out. James Dean and Marlon Brando were his favourite actors, we wanted to be just like them, and I think he could've been a good actor if someone had given him the opportunity.

Was his death a complete surprise to you?
No, not completely. I saw something going on there that I was saddened by. I was shocked, and I was surprised, but when you use the word completely, then I wasn't, no.

Is there one moment that sticks in your mind the most from your days spent making movies with Elvis?
I'll always remember when Elvis sang *Can't Help Falling in Love*, because I'm a musical person and because it was such a prominent part of our relationship. He sang that to me in *Blue Hawaii* and we were both standing at opposite sides of that chair and his hand slowly reached across and took mine. I knew how strained everything was and because we just connected. Every time I hear the song it just reminds me. Also, the last time I saw him brings a lump to my throat.

When was the last time you saw either one of those movies?
You know, I never watch them. I haven't seen them in years. Every once in a while I'll see them when I'm clicking through channels, or my son calls me late at night to tell me that they're on. I like *Kid Galahad*, but I have more feelings for *Blue Hawaii* because there were so many of them doing the rounds like that movie. I think I still see *Blue Hawaii* like so many people do, and I still get fan mail about it.

It's almost like a Disney film, very sweet and colourful.
Right, it's a very simple film, a real Hollywood magical movie. I don't know if I'm reading anything into it or not because of all the feelings that were

going on during that movie. I think there's just something about that movie that other people feel besides me. The chemistry that's happening on set, they actually see and feel from the screen.

What have you actually been up to since making those great movies?
I left the business very early on because I just didn't like it. I love to sing so I did some gigs but after all the years of writing, I've just got good at it. I can't say that I've ever missed Hollywood, but I missed the work. I missed that creative part of it. I studied acting for years and years and I was really good at it but I never got to show anybody what I could do. I never got to do films that I would've loved to have done. I now have my garden, my artwork, my kids and my granddaughter. Sorry we don't have a Hollywood happy ending here (laughs).

I hear that you might be bringing out a CD?
Let's just say that if I was forty years old then maybe. I would like to preserve my music and I probably sing now better than I ever have. If someone would say to me that they had the money to do an album and that they wanted me to pick out my songs then I would love to.

And how do you think the world should remember Elvis Presley?
Oh gosh, as a really talented singer. I think that he should be remembered as just that.

Thank you so much for that wonderful straight answer Joan, and for your time in doing this interview.
Thank you, I've really enjoyed it.

" Elvis, had an individual style and he realised that as time went by. He had his own style and the way he wanted to look. **"**

Bill Belew

Bill Belew designed Elvis' glittering on-stage costumes and his personal wardrobe from 1968 until 1977. Almost every outfit you see Elvis wearing during that period was created by Bill - the sexy two-piece leather outfit from his NBC television special, his impeccable black suit and red neck tie worn for his press conference when he opened in Las Vegas and every jumpsuit from the first karate style suits, to the magnificent caped creations, adorned with jewels, embroidery or fringes.

Julie Mundy talked to Bill Belew while researching her book *Elvis Fashion: From Memphis to Vegas*.

How did you get your first job designing for Elvis?
I had done a job for the producers on a special with Petula Clark, which came to America, then Steve Binder the producer/director called me and said "I'm going to do a special with Elvis and I'd like you to do the wardrobe." So that's how that came about.

He was looking for fresh talent in Hollywood and, more or less, was looking for people that had come from the East Coast and had fresh ideas on how they wanted to do things.

Did you meet with Elvis straight away and discuss anything particular that he wanted?
No, Elvis placed himself in my hands and said, "Bill, you do what you do."

So, I submitted several sketches to him and he said they look great.

The main thing was what he was going to wear for the concert, which Steve wanted to build the show around. We discussed it in the office and I finally said, "I don't remember Elvis being in total black leather or a leather outfit."

I'd seen him in jackets and things like that. I had a denim outfit, which was very popular in that period. In the '60s, we were all in variations of denim and we embroidered and painted them and everything. So I took this denim outfit out to the man who was constructing Elvis' clothes and I said "Romano, I want you to duplicate this in black leather." Then I went down to a leather place in LA and what I ended up with was a cordovan leather, which is like a leather that women's gloves were made out of - its very soft and very supple - and that's what I made the suit out of and we hand stitched the yokes and things on it. So that it had that denim look about it.

What about the jumpsuits? How would you say they evolved over the years? As they started off fairly plain, karate-style, and then went on to be bigger and brighter.
When I started out designing for Elvis when he first appeared in Las Vegas, the only thing that came to my mind was that I didn't want him to be the typical Las Vegas show person. So I sculpted the clothes so that they enhanced his performance.

As the time went on the fans were instrumental in leading me as to how everything evolved. As we got into it, you'll notice that they began to be more elaborate, with the embroidery work and then the jewels. By the time I got to the jewels I felt that we had made a statement about Elvis' masculinity so I didn't have to worry about it anymore.

Also, I didn't want him to be, well to quote it, 'a Liberace type person.' So I started out simple and we built on that, but the fans really dictated where we went because they demanded more opulent things from him and he was willing to go along with it.

If you could pick a favourite suit from those you created, what design would you pick?
I have two. I have the peacock suit and I have the dragon.

What about the story we've heard about the *Aloha From Hawaii* show, where you had to fly an extra cape and belt in?
I got a call from Joe Esposito and he said "Bill you are not going to believe what happened! Elvis gave away the cape and the belt!" and I said "What! We've got to get on to it right away and duplicate it." So we did. We worked all night long and I went to the belt maker and fortunately we had enough eagles to duplicate that and Nicky who owned Pzazz where I had all the beading and punching done spent all night duplicating the cape. I got grey hair from that!

You worked on a lot of personal clothes for Elvis. I would say that nearly everything I found at Graceland was your design.
He really had a great body, Julie, to design for. I've always said that Bob Mackie had Cher and I had Elvis!

He said "Billy, its hard for me to get wardrobe and I'm always given clothes, and I end up giving them to my guys. Would you design my personal wardrobe for me?"

He had like a 42" chest and his waist fluctuated from 30 to 32", so it was a great body to design for but it was out of proportion and he was also broad shouldered.

Going by his shape then, what cut and style would suit Elvis?
The cut would be 42" then we had to nip in the waist and extend the shoulders a little bit. The main thing that I said to him, which had been a feature that evolved from the jumpsuits, is that I wanted to maintain the Napoleonic collar that I designed for him so I said lets keep that as a basic for the wardrobe.

Let me ask you about Elvis' wonderful capes, how did they make first make an appearance?
Well, we were looking for a gimmick and I must, in all sincerity, say that it was Priscilla who sprung the idea. She had gone to Rodeo Drive and bought a black leather cape for Elvis and he said "Bill, let me show you something that Priscilla bought for me," and he modelled it for me and I said "Elvis this is the gimmick we have been looking for... Thanks to Priscilla I think this is it!" And that's how it evolved.

You mentioned a name earlier, and I saw on your sketch at Graceland for the black leather suit from the '68 special that you made notes for Romano. Did he work for you?
How that actually came about was that IC stood for Ice Capades. I knew the fabric that I wanted to use for Elvis, which I could only get for ice skaters. It was a stretch gabardine and it was made in Milan. I remember, I tried to buy it from another manufacturer and you had to buy like 500 yards and nobody could use that amount of any colour fabric.

I think that was the year the making of his clothes boomed, so Ice Capades decided to make a subsidiary called IC Costume. So that's how that came about. The tailor worked for Ice Capades.

So you, as Bill Belew, designed the clothes and Ice Capades made them up and later became IC Costume. What was Gene Douchette's involvement?
He worked for Nicky at Pzazz and did all the beading and embroidery work for me.

Did any of Elvis' guys come to you with their own designs for Elvis? Some of them claim to have deigned some of his clothes.
No. My association was strictly with Elvis. I dealt with the Colonel only at the beginning when he called to say that Elvis was going to open in Vegas and he would like me to do the clothes. They were pleased with what I had done for the '68 special.

How would you describe Elvis' imagination in clothes?
I think that in all the time I worked for Elvis, that he had an individual style and he realised that as time went by. He had his own style and the way he wanted to look.

We've taken a lot of photography of all the clothes for *Elvis Fashion*. Hopefully, its going to look really good. The is the first time the outfits, which are mainly all yours, have been taken out and photographed this way, so this should be a nice looking book.
Terrific! In my old age I shall finally see it! It was very exciting the first time I went to Graceland to see these things again. I was working with Todd Morgan and he was very kind to take me round and he said there was tons of stuff in the back rooms there at Graceland and I often wonder what could be in those back rooms still. It will be nice, Julie, to see it again.

I must ask about the linings. The colours of Elvis' suits were quite solid on the outside, then they had these really wild linings that surprised me.

I have a thing about linings in suits. Thank God he never complained about them when I finally finished them! I like a bit of colour.

They look fantastic. In fact, every time I saw a new suit I rushed to check the lining! People just don't see those things in photos.
No. The only person that I have seen using that nowadays is Machismo. He will once in a while do something with his linings, but I must say we were the only ones that did it then.

I must say though. Maybe five years ago there was an article in Esquire magazine by Versace and he said that "The one person I envied was Bill Belew. I would have given anything to design for Elvis." And I thought: Well! My God Versace! Then I thought... I wonder what he would have done?

❝ Elvis showered us with gifts our first morning at Graceland. I did not know what a rock star was that day, but I knew who Santa was. I just didn't know he had sideburns! **❞**

David Stanley

Can you tell me about your earliest memory of Elvis Presley?

When I moved into Graceland in early 1960 was my first memory of Elvis. Vernon, my mother Dee, my two older brothers Ricky and Billy, and myself walked in the front door and were met by Elvis. He was twenty-five years old and had just got home from Germany. He came over to us and bent down on one knee and gave us each a big hug and said "Welcome to my family, I always wanted a little brother, now I have three." That hug felt very good to me, a four-year-old little boy who had no idea what had happened to his father.

That moment defined my relationship with Elvis and in the years that followed he became more than a big brother. He was a father, mentor, friend and a person who accepted me when no one else was there to turn to.

Elvis knew that my brothers and I were victims of circumstance. And he knew that us becoming part of his family was not something we had any control over. That's why he accepted us as he did. He showered us with gifts our first morning at Graceland. I did not know what a rock star was that day, but I knew who Santa was. I just didn't know he had side burns!

Were you aware of your mother's relationship with his father back then?

No I was not. I was just a baby in 1959 when Vernon and Dee developed their relationship. Mom spoke little about it, and when she did she said their parting was a result of my dad's drinking too much. Sometimes Elvis would speak of my father. Elvis had a lot of respect for my dad because he was a WWII combat veteran and career army soldier. It was not until my father's death in 1991 that I got his side of what really happened. He left me his memoirs detailing the events that cost him his family, career and his honour. I am currently writing a book and screenplay concerning those years in 1959 and 1960 entitled *Restoring My Father's Honour*. More info on the project is available on my website.

Do you recall how Vernon behaved towards you and your brothers?

Vernon was good to us boys - the family spent a lot of time together. He drove us to school, give us our lunch monies, supported our interests. We took summer vacations together as a family. He taught us the difference in right and wrong and to respect our elders. He was a good father to me when I was growing up.

How did the move to Graceland affect you?

Let me put it to you this way. I got a lot of attention being driven to school in a pink Cadillac. Being Elvis' little brother was difficult at times both then and now. Growing up in such a surrealistic atmosphere did have an effect on me. People could be cruel. As a kid, other boys and girls would make fun of me. They would call me names like hound dog boy or sideburns. As a result of this I became very inward and very non-trusting of people. I often did not know who liked me because I was David Stanley, or because I was Elvis' little brother. As a result, I bottled up a lot of emotion and anger. And of course I found myself in trouble.

The only person that really seemed to understand was Elvis. He always told me to be myself and that people are going to be jealous of who I am. He told me that I needed to harness my anger and put the energy it created into something positive. Elvis had a lot of experience dealing with jealous people, so I have always tried to hold and practice his advice.

Sounds like good advice. What was life like at Graceland when you were a child?
My childhood days at Graceland were like being at Disneyland every day. There was always something to do when Elvis was in town. We would ride horses, race go-carts, have firework wars and play and play and then after that we would play some more.

Holidays were always special. The whole family would be together. They were great times.

Did you see Elvis much during the movie years?
Not much during school months. But in the summer Vernon, Dee, my brother and myself would spend long days on the back lots of movie studios. My first experience with Elvis and filmmaking

came in 1961 when he was filming *Follow That Dream* on location in Florida. We spent the whole summer with Elvis and the guys. It was so cool. Summer of 1967 was another great time on the sets with Elvis. He was shooting *Speedway*. During that time we had full rein of the back lot at MGM. One day my bother Billy and myself were riding on a double bicycle around the lot and ran right into a shoot of a of a TV series being done. The director yelled "Cut! What the hell do you boys think you're doing?" He was very mad. When Billy and I told Elvis about it, he did not like it that the director yelled at us. He went over to the set and told the director that he'd better not raise his voice to his little bothers again. Of course, Billy and I felt real cool. Needless to say the director apologised!

What are your memories of Priscilla in the 1960s?

That she was so pretty. I was seven-years-old when she came over and she was my first crush. She was young and very sweet. We had a lot of great times in the '60s. While Elvis was out in LA making movies, we would play a lot. She used to put on black clothes and with her dark make-up and hair she would play like Dracula and chase us boys around Graceland at night. When Elvis was in town the two of them included me in some of the fun too. We spent a lot of time by the pool, riding horses, golf carts and things like that. I recently saw some really cool footage of Elvis, Priscilla, Lisa and myself riding and playing on a golf cart in the official DVD / video *Elvis Presley's Graceland*. It brought back some great memories.

That's a great piece of footage. I guess you were at Graceland when Lisa was born, right?

Yes I was. Everyone was happy for Elvis and Priscilla. I remember the first time I saw her. My bothers and I were sitting on a couch at Graceland talking when Priscilla and Elvis brought Lisa to see us. She was an angel. As Priscilla handed Lisa to Ricky Elvis said, "Look at what God has given me." He was so proud. It truly was a wonderful moment.

Tell me about the 1968 TV special - his comeback?

The only thing I can say is we all watched it at Graceland it was an event - he showed the other rockers of the world that he was still the King. In one night he recaptured the throne. Elvis used to say to me "I have been wrong for so long, but I am right tonight." That was one of those nights!

Was there a big change in Elvis at this time?

He was happy because he was challenged and he was in the spotlight. That's where he wanted to be.

How did the split from Priscilla affect him?

Even though he knew that it was his actions that pushed her away, he considered it a great loss. He loved Priscilla, but his problem was that he loved his lifestyle more. It is no secret that Elvis was unfaithful to her. Elvis loved women and he loved having fun with his entourage. Red, Sonny, Joe, Charlie, Lamar, Marty and the others. They were Elvis' life long friends and he loved hanging out with them. It was hard for Priscilla, and it was more than she could handle. Yes, it hurt him, especially his ego.

What's your opinion on the various women Elvis dated in the '70s?

God, he had some babes! Sheila Ryan, Ann Pennington to name a few, but the one that was real to him was Linda Thompson. They had the real deal. They loved each other and you could clearly see it. But in the end she was like Priscilla, Linda could not compete with Elvis' lifestyle.

Did you ever feel that the obsessions with law enforcement and guns were a little odd?

No. There are a lot of gun collectors around the world and Elvis just so happened to be one of them. He had a great collection. As far as law enforcement is concerned, I think Elvis, like all little boys, wanted to be in law enforcement. His involvement was nothing more than a fulfilment of a little boy's dream.

What was life as a bodyguard really like?

I started working for Elvis on June 6th, 1972 when I was just 16. Elvis told me that he wanted to groom me to be a bodyguard. I had grown up around Red and Sonny West, who both left a strong impression on me. I wanted to be just like Sonny West. Big, strong, aggressive and very cool. I watched Sonny while on those early tours and absorbed as much as I could.

I also began training in the martial

❝ *I can't speak for the other guys. I can just say that I was a young rock and roller. I smoked pot and did a fair amount of substance. But I lived to tell about it. I no longer go down the road of drug use. But I won't deny the fact that I did.*❞

arts with Elvis' personal karate instructors Ed Parker and Dave Hebler. Red, Sonny, Dave Hebler, Ed Parker, Elvis and myself would spend countless hours working out on and off the road. I learned a lot about guns from Dick Grob, another member of Elvis' security team. Over time Elvis saw I was ready.

At 19, I was a black belt in karate and was carrying a 9mm automatic. I would be with Elvis everywhere he went. He nicknamed me the Headhunter because of my aggression and willingness to do whatever it took to protect him. After Red, Sonny and Dave left, my responsibilities increased. It was a lot of responsibility for a guy my age. But I can say this - no one was going to get to Elvis as long as I was with him - and no one ever did.

Any scary moments on the road?
We were coming out of a hotel during a tour and I saw a man move out of the crowd towards Elvis. He appeared to have a knife. I did not think - I moved in front of the man, pulled my gun out slammed it against his face and pushed him up against the wall. Elvis and the rest of the guys kept moving. They got

Elvis in the car and sped away. I was ready to put this guy down. The police had to pull me off him. A lot of people ask me why would Elvis need bodyguards. One just has to take a look at what happened to John Lennon to answer that question.

Yes, that was an awful loss. On a brighter note, can you give us a story regarding Elvis' generosity?
While buying a car for himself, he had me go get a poor black lady who was looking through the window of the dealership. When she came in, he said to her "Pick the one you want and it is yours." The expression on the poor lady's face said it all. Elvis made dreams come true for people whose dreams had been shattered by the realities of unfortunate circumstances. In that moment that lady saw that there was still good in the world.

What about the other guys? Who were the ones who really cared?
I think they all really cared. Understand that all the guys with Elvis were hand picked by him. You were with Elvis because he wanted you with him. Red West, Sonny West, Lamar Fike, Joe Esposito, Charlie Hodge, Marty Lacker, Larry Geller, Billy Smith, Jerry Schilling and the others were all close to Elvis. I think since Elvis passed away, there has been this thing among the people who knew Elvis concerning who knew him best, or who did he like best. Elvis loved all the guys and was close to all of them in different ways. Oh, there were the ones who came and went because their intentions were less than honourable. But let's not waste time talking about them. All I can tell you is if you were with Elvis as long as most of the guys were, you really cared for him. I was the youngest of this group. I did not go to work for Elvis until 1972 - Sure I lived around him 12 years before I started touring with him, but I knew the guys I just mentioned had more in common with him than I did. What I am

trying to say, is we all loved him very much, not because he was the King, but because he was our friend and family.

When did you notice a serious decline in Elvis' health?

I noticed it soon after I went to work for him. He was dependent on a lot of medications. But it was not until after we did the *Aloha* special that I saw it taking control of him. I could see that legitimate use of medication was turning to abuse. In the years that followed, that abuse increased to the point to where it took control of his life and ultimately lead to his untimely death.

Was there anything more anyone around Elvis could've done? What about Vernon or the Colonel?

Dave Hebler, who co-authored *Elvis: What Happened?* along with Red and Sonny West said it best in an interview seen in *This is Elvis:* "How do you protect a man from himself." No one could stop Elvis.

I must say this: So many people say to me and the other guys, if you loved him you should have stopped him. Like I said, no one could. Many tell me how much they loved Elvis and how much he meant to them and I think it is wonderful. But know this, before you judge those of us who really knew him. We saw the problems, we felt the pain first hand of having to watch a man we loved dearly go on a self destruct. We dealt with the horrors and hurts of Elvis' medication problems and we did our best to protect him and his image along the way. So before you criticize and abuse us with your harsh words remember this. We lived and saw all the things that Elvis was and did, both good and bad and we loved him anyway. When you can love a person for who and what they are, no matter what, then you are truly a fan. Believe it or not, Elvis was just a person who had faults. But in-spite of those faults he had family and friends who stuck with him right to the end.

What's the true story of you being at Graceland with a friend the day Elvis died?

Thank you for asking that - In a book done by a couple of guys who did not even know Elvis concerning his death, they said I was with a girl fooling around. Like much of the stuff written in their book, that is not true.

At the time of Elvis' death, I was living with two friends of mine, Aurelia Yarbrough and Shelly White. They were hairdressers who would do Elvis' hair from time to time. Shelly had a brother in town from Baton Rouge, LA. When I went to Graceland that day, I asked Mark White, my roommates' brother, if he would like to tag along. It was around noon on the 16th.

We were scheduled to leave that night for a tour that was to open in Portland, Maine. Elvis would not be getting up until four or so. I knew I had some time to spare so Mark and I went downstairs at Graceland and began shooting pool. Not long afterwards, a little girl named Amber (Ginger Alden's niece), who was there playing with Lisa Marie, said that Elvis was sick. I could hear the commotion going on upstairs in the living room.

My first thought was that Elvis is sick, so we may have to cancel the tour. I told Mark that I needed to take him back to the house around the corner. We headed up from the basement, jumped in my car and I rushed him home.

Upon coming back to Graceland, I saw an ambulance pull in the gate just ahead of me. That's when I realised that this was serious. The ambulance went to the front door and I went around to the back.

I jumped out of my car, ran through the house and up the stairs to Elvis' dressing room. Just as I came in one door, one of the paramedics came in another. I looked down and saw the sight that stays with me to this day. Elvis was lying in a foetal position. Joe Esposito, Charlie Hodge and Al Strada

in. With my window down, they asked what was up. I yelled out, "I think Elvis is dead" and rushed to the hospital. Upon arrival, Billy Smith and I were escorted to a trauma room where we found Joe, Charlie and Al. Elvis was in a connecting room being worked on by the doctors. Then Dr. Nick appeared, his head low and gave us the news. Elvis was gone. That was the longest, saddest day of my life.

Wow! That's a heavy story! There have been speculations surrounding drug use in the camp.
I can't speak for the other guys. I can just say that I was a young rock and roller. I smoked pot and did a fair amount of substance. But I lived to tell about it. I no longer go down the road of drug use. But I won't deny the fact that I did.

That's an honest answer - thanks. So, how has losing Elvis affected your life?
I lived a part of history. For the rest of life my name will be associated with Elvis Presley. I became his stepbrother as a result of circumstances. Circumstances I had no control over. I loved him more than anybody I have ever known, and always will.

Remember, he was no King to me. He was a man who picked me up when I was a four-year-old confused little boy and accepted me as part of his family. A lot of things can, and have, been taken away from me. Nobody can take that away from me.

were gathered around him. Joe rolled him over and we could all see that the situation was desperate. Joe began working on Elvis as the paramedics moved in to help. Everyone moved back to let them do their job. Vernon was slumped, leaning against the wall crying "Son, please don't go, please don't leave me." His friend Sandy Miller was by his side trying to comfort him. After a few moments, the paramedics motioned us to help put Elvis on the stretcher. As I grabbed Elvis to move him, Vernon placed his hand on mine and said "Feel him David, my baby is gone."

I just kept moving. We carried Elvis down the steps and placed him in the ambulance. At that moment Dr. Nick pulled up, got out of his car and jumped in the ambulance along with Joe, Charlie and Al.

I ran through the house, out the back door where I ran into Billy Smith. I told Billy the situation and he and I got into my car and headed for the hospital. On our way out the gate, Dick Grob and Sam Thompson were coming

Here's a tough one: Your mother has said some pretty controversial things about Elvis, especially shocking was the allegation that he had intercourse with his own mother. What are your views on what she has said?
That was a very bad situation for my family. My bothers and I were shocked about what she communicated to the media. As far as what I think of her views. All I can say is I have no views on it - I never heard anything about it

until I, like most people, saw it the press. I love my mother and we all have made mistakes. I know she regrets saying it. I will say this - I don't believe what she said is true.

What's your most vivid memory of Elvis, if you could chose just one?

Personally, the day he picked me up and welcomed me into his family.

Professionally, that night in 1969 when he walked out on stage in Las Vegas and defined his position as the King of Rock 'n' Roll. You had the Stones, the Beatles, the Who, Led Zeppelin and the rest dominating the world of rock 'n' roll. Then, on that night, when Elvis came out on that stage, my fourteen-year-old face lit up as I clearly then and there understood why Elvis was crowned the undisputed King of Rock 'n' Roll. Equally as cool was the fact that he was my big brother. I was so proud.

What's been happening in your life since 1977?

Well, it has taken many years to adjust to life without Elvis. He was all I knew and just like that he was gone. I was hurt, sad and yes even angered by him leaving me the way he did. As a result, I have said things about him I wish I had not said. And to the other family members and fans I say I am truly sorry for those things.

As I have grown older I have come to terms with the time that I have had to spend without Elvis. If I could do things differently during the last twenty-five years I would. The things I have said out of anger and hurt toward him, I would replace with all the good and wonderful things that made Elvis so great.

I live in Dallas, Texas now. I have a successful public relations and media consulting company. In addition I have recently created a production company where I have

written and am currently developing my first two major film projects entitled *The Headhunter* and *Restoring My Father's Honour* (www.impellofilms.com).

I spend a lot of time with my two teenage sons, Austin Aaron and Tyler. They love to tell their friends about their daddy's days with Elvis. Twenty-five years after Elvis left, he is still, and will always be, a big part of my life.

And finally, how do you think we should remember Elvis Presley?

As the King of Rock 'n' Roll, and a man who had a positive affect in the world we live in. He was a man not a Saviour - He was soul, not a saint - He was, and is, an inspiration to millions - he was a big brother, mentor and friend to me... And there is not a day that goes by that I don't think about him and miss him dearly.

David, thank you so much for such an interesting interview. I appreciate your time. It's a pleasure Polly.

Interview by Polly Hearn

"Elvis loved fellowship, he loved people... We certainly enjoyed our private moments and that was contentment."

Susan Henning

Please begin by telling us a bit about your background...
I was born in North Hollywood in 1947, my mother came from Sweden and immigrated to Ellis Island in New York with many dreams during the early 1920s

My parents moved around a little and ended up in South California where Mum went to work for a Beverly Hills salon. They were having a fashion show, a runway show, and needed two little girls. Mother jumped at the chance for my sister and I to participate and in the audience was a talent scout who later asked my mother if he could represent us for television, commercials, etc. We were signed up as of that moment so I've been working since I was six years old!

We did runway shows then we did some printwork for fashion and then I started doing television commercials which was really my speciality; I had the all American look to present a product, I was quick to pick up camera angles and it was really my gift. My sister had a knack for acting and went off to make a series of pilots for TV serials and then films. I started going into television specials, I did Dean Martin, Frankie Avalon, pretty much all of the celebrities, I was on their specials at some time. Then on to films, I did the Disney Movie *The Parent Trap* with Hayley Mills. I was the other twin in that movie actually. There's a new DVD been released that explains the real

behind the scenes story. Disney had put in my contract never to speak that there was actually another girl, that there were actually two of us playing the role. Now, after thirty years of silence I'm able to talk about it!

Following that I did another few films and then got a call to go for the interview for the Elvis film. I remember en-route to the interview my car brakes failed and I hit the car in front of me, who hit the car in front of it, making me late - not a good start to the interview!

Were you a fan of Elvis and his music at that time?
Certainly, I liked his deep voice and thought he was quite handsome but having been brought up in the business I dated many actors and in fact had married an actor prior to meeting Elvis. At the time, it was just another movie.

What do you remember about the first time you met Elvis?
A couple of days after the interview I went to wardrobe where I was wearing a mermaid tail and appeared to be topless but there were little pasties on my breasts so there was no chance of being exposed!

The first time I met him was on location at Marine World. Due to the tail, I couldn't walk, so they put me in a wheelchair. They wheeled me down for my moment and Elvis was already on the set. We introduced each other and I have to say there was an instant spark between both of us.

Sure, I liked his music but there was never any contemplation of desiring him

for a boyfriend. But the spark happened, we did the shoot and afterwards he asked if I would like to take a ride with him on the Marine World Tower. Sure, he appealed to me! Marine World was shut for us to do the film. He did bring Joe Esposito with him, which at the time I thought was strange... Why couldn't we go together? Who is this person?

The three of us went in the elevator and up the 100ft tower and we just twirled around looking out to the coast and the ocean, we had a lot of fun, we talked a lot and sparks united. He asked if he could have my number, which I gave him, the date concluded and we went our separate ways.

And Elvis called, right?

Yes, a week or two later the phone rang and it was Elvis. He said "Would you like to fly out and have a vacation with me?"

I said "Well I would, but let me think about it and call me back."

At the time I was actually engaged to a wonderful man, we'd been together for a couple of years. Being a forthright person I had a problem now. I called my fiancé and said, "You know, I'm not sure I'm not jumping too quickly into this." I was only around twenty-one and felt I may have been getting married too soon. I told him quite frankly that Elvis had called and he makes my heart go pitter-patter. I'd like to date him and if he's not the one then we could get back together. Well, this man had a lot of integrity and he said go ahead but if you're checking me out anyway, that relationship was over. But I still had that pitter-patter in my heart and if I had really loved him, I wouldn't have felt that for someone else.

Elvis called back and said, "What do you think? Would you like to fly out and meet me? I'm in Arizona, you could stay a few days."

I said, "Yeah, that sounds like fun." He sent his plane to pick me up and we were off together.

And when you arrived...?

I was treated like a princess, I took a limo and they took me to the hotel where he was at, there we met and had a wonderful time.

People magazine did a spread on Elvis' past romances and they naturally have to celebrate it. They put in there that we were in the bedroom for three days; that's incorrect, it wasn't that way. It was very difficult for him to socialise. His room was a suite (like an entire apartment). We stayed in there for three days because his entertainment was to be alone, or his buddies would come in and we'd have our meals in there. We did spend three or four days in there but it wasn't locked in the bedroom like they made it sound. That's where we were most comfortable without going out into the population of fans.

It was a good time, I learned a lot about him. We talked endlessly and just enjoyed each other as two people would.

You had a lot of laughs messing around with his hair!

Yeah, I don't think anybody else ever did that! He had long hair, you could do it in so many styles. When we were alone I'd comb it into many different styles; over to one side like the Beach Boys, or middle parting, or bangs, I'd just do funny things. Then he'd look over in the mirror and he'd laugh! It was if no-one had played with his hair before. I'd do the styles, then he'd look in the mirror and we'd laugh. It sounds so silly but some of our best memories was playing with his hair, just alone together having fun.

What was he like behind closed doors?

I know people have met him at different times, there were no drugs when I met him, I would not be in that situation for anybody.

He was a very deep person, when we talked he would go into some deep, deep philosophical conversations. He had a great sense of humour! His music was

who he was so he'd often break into song or the guys would come in and we'd sit and sing. And we laughed so much. Because of the depth of his person, it was difficult for him to be a celebrity because he couldn't be who he would've really liked to be. He loved fellowship, he loved people, he was secure with a lot of people. We certainly enjoyed our private moments and that was contentment.

It seemed like he took who he had to be very seriously. He never let anybody down, if you had Elvis performing - you were gonna get his best performance.

Alone, it was enjoyable, very stimulating brainwise. He was very, very satisfying to be with.

What happened after the holiday?
I had a daughter at that time, Courtney was three-years-old, so I had to get back home for her. We dated periodically in between and then we didn't date for months. Elvis was working on another film and I was working as an actress on other jobs.

Then I was sent out on another interview at NBC. When you go for an interview they'll tell you only a little about the project, they said it was Elvis' comeback special. They interviewed me, liked what they saw and invited me to attend rehearsals the next day. Elvis didn't know I was going to be on the show.

Meeting him again was real fun... Elvis was in the choreograph room, standing with his back to me. I walked up behind him and put my leg from behind [in between his legs] and kinda twirled it; I was wearing a leotard dance suit with bare legs. As the leg came between his, circling, he responded with his favourite saying, "My boy, my boy!" Then he turned around laughing, we had a great reunion. It was cute.

We were pleased to work together again. The sparks! I have to say there was great chemistry between us. So we did our rehearsal and he asked if I would be his support system and stay around for the duration of filming.

During some of the candid work where he's seated, wearing the black suit, you'll see him looking off to the side - that's towards me standing there in the wings, winking and supporting him.

Were you aware of the new edition of the '68 special, which is being released on DVD very soon?
No I wasn't, but I'd love to see it!

The chemistry between you two was particularly apparent in the now famous outtake scenes. Have you seen the clips?
Not all of the clips, no. Joe Esposito was here a few years ago and he brought a few that I'd never seen.

I'm sure you'll be pleasantly surprised when the DVD is released. What do you remember about filming those scenes?
We felt compatible together but I guess its becoming known to me that it was quite steamy. We were just playing around, having fun together. It was natural, we were so comfortable together.

What were you whispering to each other during the grape scenes...?
"Mmmm... Reminds me of Phoenix," and "Wait 'til the cameras stop rolling..." Whatever was required to serve a scene, we were both professionals doing a job and so you give them what they want to see. It was all about keeping ourselves motivated to give them what they needed to photograph.

How was Elvis during filming of the special, was he nervous?
I think he was a little apprehensive, he was a very humble person and sometimes he'd seem insecure - until he started singing and that would overtake any questions about himself and his self-confidence. Certainly there was apprehension, although he didn't articulate his fears, it was apparent.

As the special began to evolve into its own being you could tell then it would be a success. Everything was flowing. Steve Binder, the director, was just outstanding in getting the best out of Elvis. It was a great working team.

And the Colonel, did you meet him?
I only met him a few times, he was like the overseer to ensure that things were going in the best interests of his client. He was a little on the dry side, certainly polite but he didn't show much emotion. He was not someone that you'd run up and hug, not really a warm person.

You mentioned Joe Esposito, do you remember any of the other guys?
Yes one, what was his name....? Dark hair. I can't remember right now. They all worshipped Elvis, they all enjoyed being around him even if it hadn't been a job. They were wonderful. There was such a unity in the group. I'm sure that when they took the job they took it because you couldn't help but love Elvis.

He was very, very good to them, very considerate. He treated them respectfully. I have a farm now and have many employees working for me. One thing that Elvis taught me was that we are all just human beings and some of us are in different positions but it doesn't mean that you're better than anybody. He always treated everybody with equal respect.

Was Priscilla ever around the set?
No. Never. I hadn't really followed his marital status, but when I told my mother I was dating Elvis she said "He's married!" When I saw him I said "Mom says you're married?" and I wanted some clarity, I'd heard it was on again, off again. He said although they were still legally married they had separated and he would be seeking a divorce. I wouldn't date married men per se.

Now, as a more mature woman, I would say wait until it's done and we can talk about it but I guess at that time when put in the situation where he tells me that.... I'm still just a human being! (laughs) But it wasn't as if he and Priscilla were a romantic couple.

I've heard it said that Elvis chose not to be intimate with women who had children. What are your thoughts on that?
We had no problem with intimacy! I hadn't heard that. In fact our daughters were born around the same time. This certainly didn't inhibit our relationship whatsoever.

Since my profession was my body, three months after my daughter was born I did some bikini shots. I've always been very athletic and maintain my body to a good standard.

Having never known him without a child, I can say there was nothing more that I would've wanted from him. There was nothing I would've changed about our relationship.

What happened after filming of the special had concluded? Did you see Elvis again?
Yeah, I flew to Vegas a few times. He would invite me, I never sought after him, I don't do that. We dated on and off. He'd call and say "Hey, you wanna come up and keep me company for a

" That we didn't end up together was a choice for the Lord and I wish his life could've gone on for him to become an old grandfather to enjoy so much more."

while?" So I would do that. The last time I saw him was in Vegas.

How did your relationship come to an end?
I got into another relationship and that was the end of that. When I started dating him, the person I ended up marrying.

I had a direction where I was going, I wanted to be into horses. If you live with an actor (I had already done that once) you very much live for them and their life. And it wasn't the direction I chose to go.

I met my husband, who was a dressage rider from Holland, and it was a wrong telephone number that put us together. We met later after talking on the phone for three months. I started feeling that I was falling in love. He is very much my best friend. We're united in a journey

It came to a natural conclusion with Elvis but I think it was best for both of us. I don't know for both of us, but it certainly was the best direction for my life at that time.

What do you recall of the time that Elvis died?
I was in Canada and I was married to my second husband, I was up in this tall tower, a hotel overlooking Spruce Meadows and my husband was in meetings. I was talking to my father, who was very much a fan of Elvis, he loved the music and what Elvis

represented, I think there were some latent desires in my father that Elvis fulfilled that my father could not. I think he was the most excited when I was dating Elvis. My father called and said "Honey, have you heard the news?" and he told me. I remember looking out the window, and it struck us both so hard. There were many hours that I was alone in the hotel and I dwelled on the memories, it was a wonderful time to be alone to cry and to pray and really absorb the impact of how this is going to affect the world. And now of course I'm so appreciative that his memory did not die with him but has been kept alive for the generations. He truly is an icon, not just of the music industry, but I think an era.

I disdain when people bring the bad out or the short periods that... I don't know, I wasn't part of it, but any negative in his life. I resent that. Of the good, it was one millionth that perhaps had gone awry, but the good... that man changed the world. This world would be different if there never was an Elvis in it.

How do you think he should be remembered?

Certainly an instigator in true rock 'n' roll. An instigator in the music industry and his songs can hold a candle right now to the greatest music, his music will never die. As long as the world has music, they'll be there.

For the person he was, the character. He didn't fall into the Hollywood trap of changing himself. He was true to himself and his faith.

What are you doing now, thirty-six years after the television special?

I'm living my dream: 82 horses and 112 acres. I live and breathe horses all day. I still do a little acting, I did a show with Brooke Shields not too long ago. Just a small part but it was fun. I don't do interviews any more, but if someone calls and wants me then I'll think about it. My life is on a path that is really

satisfying, not that the acting business isn't, it is a bit more shallow. My eldest daughter was involved in the business for a while and I have two other children that I'd like to keep out of the business.

How would you like to close, anything you'd like to add?

I have nothing but respect for him and he'll forever have a part of my heart. That we didn't end up together was a choice for the Lord and I wish his life could've gone on for him to become an old grandfather to enjoy so much more. I will always hold him alive in my heart. I'm sure he's up there overlooking all of this.

I'm just glad that Priscilla and his daughter have chosen to share these quiet moments that haven't been seen, the more we can learn more about him and share it with the world. I think that makes him more alive.

Susan, thank you very much for taking the time to speak with me today.

Diane, speaking with you has been a pleasure, you have the most beautiful accent! I'm glad I'm able to and it makes my life a little more enriched sharing these memories with you. This has brought it back to life for me, pleasant memories that were in my past. I didn't realise at the time I was part of history and now, in retrospect, fun to be part of history. At the time he was a boyfriend, but looking back on my life I realise it was a wonderful event in my life to have known him and had those special times we enjoyed together. I enjoyed it then and appreciate it now.

Interview by Diane Johnston

" When it came to religion and spiritual matters, Elvis' insights were quite profound. He always brought his humour and his exceptional philosophic insights into whatever he did, especially his music. "

Larry Geller

Larry Geller was Elvis' close friend and hairdresser. His interest in religion and the occult interested Elvis and the two spent many hours reading and talking about the supernatural and all things strange. Elvis called him 'the Guru' during those fourteen years of friendship and Larry has always remained supportive of the King. Here's a short but interesting account of those times as recorded by Andrew Hearn....

Hi Larry, thanks for your time.
Hi Andrew. To begin with, I want to thank you very much for giving me the opportunity to share with you and your magazine readers some of my experiences and memories with my close friend Elvis Presley. I'll do my best to answer the questions you ask, some of my responses might surprise you, and as you read further you will see that I take this subject very seriously. As you know, there have been certain people who have made some very disturbing claims and have spread false stories.

Firstly, can I clear something up? I was once given a lock of Elvis' hair which I was told originally came from a guy called Holmer Gilliland who often cut Elvis' hair. What's your view on this Larry?
This person Holmer Gilliland didn't have any of Elvis' hair strands. I believe you were ripped off. Any time Elvis' hair was cut it was immediately thrown away so that very thing would never occur.

Elvis always saw to it that his hair would not be exploited. However, when Charlie Hodge went with me to the funeral parlour where I attended to Elvis hair the day after he died, I purposely removed the hair that I cut that dreadful morning, and kept it. There is no way I'd ever sell it, it was removed to stop the exploiters.

Going right back to the beginning, when did you first meet Elvis and how did you end up working for him?
I first met Elvis April 30th 1964. I was styling the hair of singing star Johnny Rivers when my phone rang. At the other end was one Alan Fortas who worked for Elvis. Alan said that Elvis heard of my work. You see, our shop was the very first men's hairstyling salon in the USA. Some of our clients included Frank Sinatra, Warren Beatty, Steve McQueen, Peter Sellers and many more of the top stars of the entertainment world.

After working on these great super stars, the thought of meeting Elvis and working on his hair was... the ultimate.

That afternoon I drove up to his home in Bel Air, on Perugia Way and we met. We went into his bathroom where

I proceeded to cut his hair for the film *Roustabout*. Elvis and I got into a very deep conversation concerning religion, spiritual growth, his twin brother Jesse Garon, his beloved mother and many other intimate details of his life. When Elvis saw that I was into the spiritual aspect of life, and I told him of many books I read, he asked right then and there to work for him full time and to give up my clientele of celebrities. Elvis and I bonded that very first meeting and I told him I would work for him full time and go back to my shop and quit, who wouldn't?

You're right. Who wouldn't quit their job to work with Elvis. So when did you go on the payroll?
The very next day at Paramount studios I was put on the payroll. Working and living with Elvis is certainly the most exciting, eventful and most significant part of my life. I travelled with him, lived at Graceland, worked with him every day for years and styled his hair for the movies, *Roustabout, Girl Happy, Tickle Me, Double Trouble, Easy Come, Easy Go, Frankie and Johnny, Paradise, Hawaiian Style, Spinout, Harum Scarum* and *Clambake*. I also took care of his hair for personal appearances, hundreds of concert tours, TV specials and of course for the very last time for his funeral.

I believe Pat Parry also cut Elvis' hair. Did you take turns?
When I groomed Elvis' hair Pat Perry nor anyone else ever took turns, it just didn't work that way. Pat only cut his hair a few times.

Going back to the movies. How did Elvis feel about doing them?
Elvis really disliked the type of movies he appeared in. He strongly felt that if he was given some real acting roles that

he would grow as an actor, and he felt he had the talent, this was one of his fondest dreams. He was very upset with his manager, Colonel Parker, for putting him in as he would often say 'teeny bopper' movies. Elvis knew all too well that he was being used.

Shortly before his death he was going to dismiss Parker and hire a new manager, stop touring and get back to acting again, only this time in some dramatic roles. Everyone around Elvis knew how he felt about this subject, it was no secret as he would often express his feelings openly.

So what was Elvis really like to be around? Was he smart?
Elvis was so fantastic to be around. His sense of humour was great, he was always making jokes, and he was so easy to work for. Another essential aspect of him, contrary to his public image, was that he was very intelligent. He was a voracious reader. I would bring him new books on a daily basis. He would spend hours each and every day reading, underlining favourite passages, and would stun people with his knowledge and understanding.

When it came to religion and spiritual matters - his favourite subject - his insights were quite profound. Elvis loved life, he enjoyed sports, movies, cars, karate and many subjects. Yet, he always brought his humour and his exceptional philosophic insights into whatever he did, especially his music.

I understand that the Colonel wasn't too keen on having you around. Why?
Now when it came to Colonel Parker and me, it is true that he didn't like my influence with Elvis. Why? Because he knew quite well that I always urged Elvis to be more independent, brought him books to open him up and give him a chance to think for himself and not be so dependant upon Parker. The Colonel was against Elvis exploring other cultures, new ways of thought and relating to life, especially when Elvis

began actively searching for truth, for God. This threatened Colonel Parker, he thought he was losing control to me.

Parker couldn't have been more mistaken. Now, I've only barely touched the tip of the iceberg here. This subject deserves a complete explanation and not part of this first interview, which is only laying the groundwork for future communication if you wish. I know that perhaps this is getting deep, only remember, you want to know the truth about Elvis and have a deeper understanding of his life and just what went on. We both have to put forth some effort here if that goal is to be reached. Elvis was very complicated, and there is so much to his life and on-going legend. The fact is; Elvis is the greatest star who ever lived.

Thanks. Perhaps we can talk again sometime?
I feel that for my first contact with you, that I've said enough and what has been said should be food for thought. In April of 1977, just a few short months before Elvis' passing, he asked me in no uncertain terms to write a book with him, to tell the world about the truth about his life, the good, the bad, the ugly and everything. He said, "The fans know Elvis all right, but they don't know me. I want to know what I'm going through, about my spiritual life and all my experiences and the books that I read, because if they don't learn about that, they'll never know the real story." I pledged to him that day in Detroit, Michigan during that tour, to help him to get his side of the story out. And his version concerning the matters already discussed are that story, the very lynchpin of the wheel. Feel free to contact me again.

Thanks Larry, I'll do that.

"I was fully aware of the magnitude of Elvis'
presence and personally -
it was a little frightening.
There was a strange aura around
this man that I cannot describe."

Jeanne LeMay

Former Miss Rhode Island Jeanne
LeMay never dated Elvis, but she played
a key part in his life. Andrew Hearn
talks to Linda Thompson's best friend
about the Elvis she knew.

Firstly, Can you tell me about your
friendship with Linda?
Linda and I first met when we were
roommates in the Miss USA pageant in
1972, she as Miss Tennessee and me as
Miss Rhode Island. We were introduced
by our chaperone at the Governor's
house in Puerto Rico. Linda said, "Hey
Rhode Island, pleased to meet ya," with
a Northern accent to poke fun at the
way I talked, and I thought how funny
she was and liked her immediately. She
was a good Christian girl who I admired
as she would read her bible every day.
She had the most fantastic personality
(she and I both were voted Miss
Congeniality in our state pageants) and
everyone loved her and wanted to be in
her company. We had a great time in
Puerto Rico and stayed two extra weeks
after the pageant. We got to be close
friends as there was never any
competition between us at all. Linda
and I talked about what we would like
to do in the future. She invited me to
move to Memphis and share an
apartment. I felt very comfortable

around her and knew she would make a
wonderful roommate. I moved there on
July 1st 1972 and we met Elvis on July
6th, so our plans changed dramatically.
She moved in with Elvis instead, and I
said to Elvis, "If she had moved in with
anyone else, I would have never forgiven
her, but considering it's you, I guess it
is okay!"

I understand Linda wasn't too keen on
meeting Elvis, but you insisted.
Yes, Linda and I were supposed to
model fur coats that night and I said,
"How many opportunities do you get to
meet Elvis Presley and we are going!" I
honestly couldn't believe we were
actually going to meet him because I
thought that Bill Browder, who invited
us to go to the Memphian Theatre, was
interested in Linda and it was just a
way of getting to score with her. Also,
coincidentally, my twin sister and I had
met Tom Jones in Rhode Island almost
a year ago to the day and I thought how
lucky can I get. It was a dream come
true.

In your own words, can you tell me
about that first night you met Elvis at the
Memphian Theatre?
Well, when we arrived, Bill Browder was
there with a girl so I knew that he
probably wasn't after Linda after all. We
were standing in the lobby and Elvis

came crashing through the doors with a black cape with red satin lining and a white shirt and I whispered to Linda that I thought he looked like Dracula, so Linda told him so. When we were introduced to him, Linda talked to him like she knew him her whole life and he was smitten. As far as we knew, he was still married but I thought Elvis was the most handsome man I had ever seen and I was thrilled to be meeting him. He had the most dreamy eyes and sensuous mouth. He was quite charming, but he was still Elvis Presley and I was fully aware of the magnitude of his presence and personally, it was a little frightening. There was a strange aura around this man that I cannot describe.

You and Linda were both beauty queens, so why do you think Elvis took an instant interest in Linda and did you feel a little disappointed that it wasn't you?
No, to be honest with you, I was initially intimidated by him. After we were introduced in the lobby, Linda and I were sitting at the end of the row of seats and George Klein came and sat in the last seat next to Linda, as he knew her well. Elvis was about ten rows in front of us surrounded by girls but he kept turning around. I think Linda said something to him like, "My aunt told me to tell you hello, she used to live in the same projects that you did." All of a sudden, Elvis got up and went to the back of the theatre and George flew out of the seat to follow. Within a minute, Elvis came and plopped down in the seat next to Linda and Linda said without hesitation, "To what do we owe this honour?" He was taken aback and almost stuttering said, "Well, I just thought that I would sit down."

I was flabbergasted and kept poking her in the ribs, as I couldn't believe she would say something like that to a superstar. But you have to understand, Linda not only is beautiful, she is extremely witty, charming, confident and so delightful to be with. Elvis admired those qualities. They shared the same cultural background, religious beliefs and sense of humour. There was no contest with Linda and I, and I never felt any jealously because Elvis fell in love with her. I was absolutely ecstatic for her good fortune.

Did you accompany Linda on any dates?
Yes, Elvis invited us to Graceland the next night, which was Friday, July 7th. When we pulled up to the house, we

were so excited to be going inside. I thought it looked very homey at the time considering who lived there. This was before he had it redecorated in 1975 which most people think is rather gaudy but Elvis had flamboyant taste and the décor reflected that. Elvis was still upstairs but when he came down, he looked great. He showed us around Graceland including the trophy room, which I found fascinating. Then he took us around the grounds on a golf cart. Red West and I sat on the back and when we went over the old cornrows, I almost fell out because he was going so fast. I had my first camera so I asked if I could take pictures. Elvis obliged and started to kiss Linda in front of the door to Graceland. Then when I stood with Elvis to get a picture (which Red took) Elvis turned and kissed me! I thought I would pass out. I know he didn't do it out of disrespect to Linda; he just loved to shock and give everybody a thrill, and let me tell you, it was! Mysteriously, the film from those pictures came out black. I assume Red West exposed the film somehow so as to protect Elvis. We then left for the Gulf Shores with Linda's family for two weeks. While we were away, Linda kept asking me if I thought he would call and I never had any doubts that he would. I am very perceptive and was positive he would contact her and when we returned, we found out he had been trying to get a hold of her the whole time.

Would you say that you had a friendship with Elvis because you were Linda's best friend, or were you genuinely fond of each other regardless?
Yes, I would say it was through Linda that I had a friendship with Elvis. One of the reasons that I remained friends with Linda is that I never made any overtures at him. It was morally wrong and I valued my friendship with her more than having a brief fling with a superstar. Don't get me wrong, I found him absolutely gorgeous and felt love and devotion to him as a friend and

admired him for his wonderful qualities; but there was no way I could have handled Elvis Presley. I just didn't have the confidence to be with someone of his stature. This is funny. Linda told me once that Elvis said, "You know, I think I know Jeanne well enough that if I made a pass at her, she would tell me to go bleep myself!" I think he respected me for my loyalty to my friends.

How would you honestly describe their overall relationship?
I think they truly loved each other and fulfilled each other's needs. They were cute and playful together with a childlike spirit. And when they joked around and laughed, it was a contagious happening. Linda was so motherly by caring for him and they had the most adorable baby talk you ever heard. It was a language all their own.

Did Linda confide in you about her love for Elvis at that time?
Linda was a sweet, innocent, southern girl and I knew that she had never been completely intimate with a man before. She did confide in me about her apprehensions of getting involved with him. She wanted to make sure he really loved her. I knew she was in love for the first time, but can you imagine the pressure of having Elvis Presley as your first serious love? I told her it was okay and I believed he really loved her. She told me I was the only person she could trust as many women would throw themselves at him behind her back. She had enough confidence to hold onto him but I know she was concerned about his little flirtations. She truly understood Elvis and knew it was a need that he had to be around women and to get that kind of adoration. But I know she loved Elvis for himself and was unquestionably the best thing that ever happened to him. Many fans have written to me and expressed their love for Linda and their gratitude to her for taking care of him. Some of them believe that if she were with him, he

would still be alive. She even saved his life a couple of times because she was so attuned to his needs. It just was not God's will and although we all miss him and wish he were still with us; I know he is in a wonderful place hopping around on the clouds. I can picture him laughing and being absolutely delighted and honoured by the overwhelming devotion. They are truly doing a wonderful job keeping his memory alive and I'd like to take this opportunity to thank them.

Did you witness both the ups and downs or did they keep this kind of thing private?
I never witnessed them fighting but when Elvis hurt Linda's feelings; she would call me at four in the morning and tell me about it. She would read me poems, which she would write when she was sad and hurt, and I would say, "My God, are you really talented, you really wrote that?" She said she had been writing poems since she was a child. I envy this innate gift and I knew she had the ability to become a great songwriter. This has become a reality as she has had great success writing songs for Celine Dion, Barbara Streisand, Whitney Houston and many other famous artists.

Tell me about the various things you did with Elvis as a group.
We mostly would go to movies at the Memphian or the karate studio or simply hang around the house. Once we went racing around the grounds on the golf carts all night long. It had snowed in Memphis the Christmas of 1973 which is infrequent, and I had taken Lisa Marie sliding for the first time in her life down the hill in the front yard of Graceland. She was such a precious little girl and I played with her on her new trampoline and told her stories. Elvis had a three-wheeler motorcycle and we would race through the gates on those. He loved his toys. I also remember how delighted I was whenever he would sing for us.

" This man was extraordinarily charismatic and attracted women like a magnet. The attitude and energy of him as a performer is incomparable."

Any funny moments that stick in your mind?
There is one in particular when he gave me a car. It was a Pontiac Ventura with a leopard top and because it was a stick shift [manual gears], which I couldn't drive, Elvis said he would show me and drive it back to Graceland. Picture this... Elvis in the drivers seat, next to him was Linda, then me. Everybody was staring at us on the road so Elvis said, "Honey, look at everybody looking at your new car."
So I said "Elvis, did you ever stop and think they could be looking at you?" And he said, "Oh yeah, I forgot about that!" He was a real person.

What about Elvis on stage? Did you see many shows and could you tell us a little more about Elvis the performer?
Yes, when I went on tour in 1973, we went to ten cities including New York, Philadelphia, Cincinnati, St. Louis, Atlanta, and Nashville. I remember having a little motion sickness on the plane. I was sitting across the aisle from where Linda and Elvis were sitting, and Elvis held my hand and did some kind of karate exercise which was suppose to relieve the symptoms. I thought how kind he was to be concerned for me and yes, it did work, but I think I was still in a state of shock at being invited on tour. When Elvis asked me to join them on the tour, he

said it was the least he could do for taking Linda away from me. Wasn't that sweet? Linda also called me when I was still living in Rhode Island and asked me to join them in Las Vegas. I had my own beautiful suite and I saw the shows every night for about a week. I also saw the show he did in Memphis in 1975 when I was working there. It was such a privilege to be in a position to attend all those shows when I knew how difficult it was to obtain tickets.

What did you personally think of him as a performer?

I was always a big fan of Elvis since the '60s and loved going to his movies and wishing I was one of the girls in it.

Every time I saw him perform on stage, it literally took my breath away. The electricity in that room was like nothing I had ever experienced in my life. This man was extraordinarily charismatic and attracted women like a magnet. The attitude and energy of him as a performer is incomparable.

Did you ever feel that Linda and Elvis would marry and possibly have children?

Yes, I did think that maybe they would marry and I know they talked about kids. I knew Linda would make a great mother and they would produce a beautiful, talented child.

Did you witness the decline in his health and how aware was Linda of such troubles?

I knew Elvis' health was declining because I was working there in the office in 1975 when he was admitted to the hospital about four or five times. I also had dated one of Elvis' doctors who told me he had a lot of physical problems and he probably wouldn't live to be very old, about fifty-five. I was stunned, to say the least. Linda confided in me that Elvis was abusing prescription drugs. She was worried and tried to get him to stop. He was getting heavy and he would eat such enormous portions of food and then starve himself with these

fad diets, which never worked for long. The last time I saw him alive, he was so heavy that I didn't even recognise him. It was a sad situation to witness the self-destruction of such a beautiful man.

Did you have any knowledge of the high usage of prescription medication by Elvis and other members of his inner circle?

Like I said, I was aware of the problem but I never witnessed Elvis or anyone around him taking any drugs, pills or anything. I know that may be hard to believe, but Linda and I didn't drink or smoke. We were both very naive concerning drugs and I had no desire to learn. Consequently, when Linda told me of Elvis' drug abuse, I realised the repercussions of the problem. I remember seeing pill bottles in the bathroom and by the bed, but I never read what the bottles contained.

Do you know about the shooting incident in Las Vegas where Linda was almost hit?

Yes, as a matter of fact, when I was in Las Vegas after the show Linda and I went to her dressing room suite and she showed me the bullet hole. Elvis was angry at some of the guys that night because of something they had failed to do, and came into the main suite and started yelling wildly and firing them all. I was so scared and said to Linda, "Get me the hell out of here before he starts shooting!"

I had witnessed him shooting one of the cars, the Pantera, when it failed to start, so I knew he wouldn't hesitate to use a gun.

Were you aware that Linda was considering a break-up?

Linda did confide in me about ending the relationship. She was becoming increasingly unhappy and frustrated with Elvis' behaviour and I knew she couldn't take much more. She got close to David Briggs, Elvis's piano player, and I had accompanied them on a couple of dates. I remember there was a song out at the time called *Torn*

Between Two Lovers. I told her she had to go with her heart but she had to think of her emotional health too. She felt helpless to stop Elvis from the abuse and the other women. She did everything for him that anyone could possibly do and more. I am sure it was the most difficult decision of her life.

You ended up working at Graceland right?
Yes, when I moved back to Memphis in 1974, I had been working as a hostess-supervisor in a restaurant and one day Linda called and said, "Elvis wants to know if you want a job doing his fan mail." I worked with Patsy [Gambill], Elvis' cousin, Paulette, and Vernon,

Elvis' dad. I really didn't see Elvis that much during the day because they were asleep. It is not like he dictated letters to us or anything. So, I handled the fan mail and also would stay at Graceland with Linda or travel with her when Elvis went out of town. That is how I had the opportunity to take pictures of the upstairs of Graceland, the bedroom, office and bathroom etc. I left in 1976 to move to Los Angeles to share the apartment, which she and Elvis had rented when they went to California

Have you been back to Graceland since?
No, I regret to say I have not been back but hope to visit someday.

Who do you remember from Elvis' guys and can you tell me how they treated you?

I remember all of them and they treated me very well, although, someone made a pass at me when I went on tour. So when Linda told Elvis, he told all the guys that I was his guest and was off limits.

Are you in touch with any of them today?

No, except that Joe (Esposito) was in Rhode Island last January promoting his book and I got to see him.

I know you and Linda are still best friends. Has she changed much over the years?

Linda still has the same wonderful personality and in my opinion, she has gotten even more beautiful throughout the years, if that is possible. She is involved in many charitable causes, which reflect her goodness and generosity. She always had the most perfect body and still does. Shopping with her is like having a human Barbie doll because everything looks good on her. I have never known anyone who can equal her warmth, sweetness, generosity, sense of humour, kindness and intelligence. She has always been my role model and I love her and think of her as my sister. I consider it a privilege to be her friend. Linda gave me a card once that read *'What made us friends in the long ago when first we met; well, I think I know. The best in me and the best in you hailed each other because they knew, that long ago since time began, our being friends was part of God's plan.'* I never forgot that.

How often do you get to see her these days?

Well, not as often as I would like. However, I was visiting with her recently, last June, at her mansion in Malibu after not seeing her for a while and it was the most joyous experience.

When the driver drove through the gate of the estate, I thought it was a park with a huge hotel. It was magnificent and totally breathtaking. Her hospitality is wonderful and she always shows me such a marvellous time. Her husband, David Foster, who is a musical genius, always entertains me with a mini concert on the piano, which is always a thrill. They are a very entertaining couple and I thoroughly enjoy being in their company. Linda is extremely talented and can think up lyrics to a song while she is on the treadmill. I am very proud and happy of her accomplishments and always believed in her ability. I feel honoured and fortunate that Linda and I are still friends after thirty years and that in spite of her success, she has not forgotten me. We try to stay in touch by calling each other as often as possible and when I hear her voice, all the memories of the past come flooding back and I feel we're twenty-one again.

Do you and Linda ever chat about those incredible years?

Yes, we talked about when we had met him and all the wonderful times we had throughout the years. There are some very fond memories but it was not a normal life style. It was a real whirlwind sometimes and other times it was like living a fairytale. When I was working there, I would work from nine to five and Linda and Elvis would be just waking up at 5pm as they stayed up all night and slept during the day. Once, when I was leaving the office, Linda was up in the barred window and she waved and appeared so pathetic. She looked like a princess who couldn't escape from her tower, so I yelled up, "Rapunzel, Rapunzel, let down your hair!" That line was from the famous fairytale about the princess with such long hair that she threw it out the window of the tower and the prince climbed up and rescued her. It was an isolated existence and wasn't always as glamourous as people imagine.

Was it a thrill to be portrayed in the movie Elvis and the Beauty Queen?
When Linda called to tell me that she was going to make me immortal, I just cracked up. It was thrilling, to say the least, especially when I witnessed some of the filming of the movie and met Don Johnson, Stephanie Zimbalist, and Ann Duesenberry who played me. When I met Ann, I said, "It is so nice to meet you and I am so glad they chose someone pretty, and I always wanted blonde hair and blue eyes. Well, Linda and the director actually doubled over laughing because they thought it was so funny watching me with this actress.

I know Don Johnson was a million miles from Elvis, but do you think the rest of the movie was fairly accurate?
Not really. Linda said she wasn't satisfied with the end result and I certainly didn't like the scene where I jump on the gate and say, "Rover, Rover, can Elvis come over?" That was so unlike anything I would have done. I told Linda recently that we should have played ourselves. It would have been hysterically funny. And I didn't like the way they portrayed Elvis and his drug abuse. I wish they had showed the real Elvis as I read the script, and they left out all the positive aspects of his personality.

When you look back on your days with Elvis, how would you describe those few years hanging out with the King?
It was the most thrilling and unforgettable experience of my life. I remember the Christmas I spent at Graceland there was an ice storm, which prevented me from returning to Rhode Island for a couple of days. Elvis, Linda and I were walking around the grounds of Graceland in this beautiful winter wonderland and I remember thanking God for allowing me this unbelievable opportunity to actually be spending the holidays with Elvis Presley.

What are you up to these days Jeanne?
I am married to a wonderful man and we bought a beautiful house (which we joking call the mini Graceland because the front of the house resembles it) with a heated, indoor pool, which is my heaven as I am an avid swimmer. I work in sales and lately I have been contemplating writing a book due to the enormous encouragement and support I have received from the fans.

Tell me about the sale of your photos and your great website.
Due to the twenty-fifth anniversary of Elvis' death, I knew that my pictures of the upstairs of Graceland would want to be seen by the fans so I started to auction them. The response was overwhelming and my husband established a website called www.elvissecretary.com. I can honestly say that it has been the most rewarding experience of my life to hear how grateful the fans are for making the pictures available to view or purchase for their collections. This has been an exciting venture and I love to read of the devotion people still have for Elvis and their stories simply touch my heart. I have learned through this how Elvis continues to reach out and touch new generations of fans around the world and it is very gratifying indeed.

And finally, how do you think Elvis should be remembered?
There is no doubt that Elvis was the greatest entertainer of the twentieth century but for those of us who were fortunate enough to know him, he was also tender, funny, generous and kind. He had frailties and idiosyncrasies that most human beings have. He should not be worshipped, but admired and respected for the magnificent talent he had and for the extraordinary man he was. He was God's gift to the world and we were truly blessed to be given the gift of hearing his voice, seeing that handsome face, and experiencing his phenomenal performances.

"Elvis would come home off the tours and he may go a week, ten days, two weeks without taking a thing. If he was addicted, he couldn't do that."

George Nichopoulos

In this, his first ever fan-based magazine interview, Elvis' friend and former physician George Nichopoulos, known simply as Dr. Nick, talks to Andrew Hearn about his time with the King...

Okay, let's start from the beginning. When did you very first meet Elvis?
George Klein's girlfriend [Barbara Little] worked in my office around 1967. I was on duty one Sunday when I got a call saying that Elvis had been riding horses at the Circle G ranch and that he was saddle sore.

So, you made the trip out to Graceland?
No, I went all the way up to the damn ranch, three times! I went all the way out there to take a look and he asked if I wouldn't mind stopping by Graceland to take a look at his grandma. I said that I was kinda on call but he insisted saying that it'd only take a minute. When I dropped by the house, I learned that he'd called ahead asking if I could go back out there because he'd forgotten to ask me something.

It's a good few miles from Graceland isn't it?
Yeah, about eight or ten miles, it's a pretty good drive. Anyway, I asked one of the maids in the kitchen if she could get him on the phone so I could talk to him, but she said he wanted to talk to me personally. So I go back out there.

It must've been pretty important to get you to drive all the way back out to the ranch again.
No. I don't recall what he asked me, something off the wall. I think he just wanted to check something. But then he wanted me to stop by the house again on the way back. So, I got back to Graceland and they said Elvis had called and he'd forgotten to ask me something. I went back a third time...

What did he want?
Nothing.

So what do you think the reasoning was behind asking you to drive out there three times?
He just liked having new people around, just someone new to talk to. He'd get tired of the same people, some of the guys. He'd get tired of their conversations too. He loved to talk about a lot of things. They'd carry three of four lockers full of books on tour just full of books. Sometimes he may not have touched any of them, but if he wanted to read, he wanted to read and he had to have them. He was very well read.

So, what happened after your extremely hectic day running to and from the ranch for Elvis?
I saw him the next day.

He called again did he?
Yeah (laughs).

When did you actually become his personal physician?
Well, as soon as he started touring he wanted me along. I told him that I just couldn't do it because I knew what would happen to me as a doctor if I did. I wouldn't be able to continue with my practice, get more schooling and do all the things I needed to do.

But you went along in the end.
Yeah, and a few times he got pissed off and tried to fire me. I told him that he couldn't fire me because I didn't work for him.

You were never on the payroll?
Never on the payroll. When I went on the tours we figured out a formula because the other doctors in my office were getting jealous, they thought it was all a vacation. We figured out what I probably would have made if I'd have stayed at home for the two weeks, three weeks or a month, and then Elvis would pay me that amount. I would then give it to them (the other doctors).

So, your boss was happy enough with the arrangement to let you go on tour?
Right.

And you looked after just Elvis?
No, a hundred and fifty people.

What kind of thing were you treating?
It depended on what state we were in and what the season was. It could be flu, diarrhoea, vomiting to venereal disease. We had one guy on the tour, Felton Jarvis, who had a kidney transplant. Before he had the transplant I went along and did dialysis with him. I had to do a lot of different stuff just for Felton.

Was it difficult to handle all those people?
The worse thing about it is that they were all night people. They slept during the day, they came alive and got sick at night.

And I guess that as soon as you came off the tour, you had to fit right back in to your normal hours at the practice?
Right, it was demanding. When we were home I'd still see Elvis probably five or six days out of the week. Every night on the way home I'd go by his house just to check on him or just to sit and talk. He loved to talk.

I want to ask you about the efforts made by doctors in Vegas to help Elvis shed some extra pounds. How did that work?
They had figured out a way for him to lose weight by putting him to sleep for three weeks at a time, just waking to take liquids. At the end of it he'd gained ten pounds!

**A good rest but not much of a diet!
What, in your opinion, was the most
serious threat to Elvis' health? Many fans
would say it was his intake of drugs.**
Some fans are really ignorant of what
really went on. Elvis had a colon
complaint where he was born without a
nerve supply to the colon and small
intestine.

A major problem was that nothing
could move through the intestine
because he didn't have the nerve to force
it through. So, Elvis' colon was just
getting bigger and bigger, it was simply
huge at the time of his autopsy. Elvis
asked why part of his colon just simply
couldn't be removed. It was this
problem that caused his big stomach.
We talked to two or three doctors but
because it was Elvis, they just wouldn't
do it. It wasn't really being done that
much in the '70s and they were scared
to do it. Today there wouldn't be a
problem. They wouldn't think twice
about it. It was serious because when
you get a build up of material in the gut
it can get septic. You might survive, or
you may die by the time the bacteria hits
the blood stream. This was the reality of
one of the illnesses that he had.

What caused Elvis' voice to slur on stage?
There was one time when I went to
Vegas or Palm Springs when Elvis got
mad at me and he cussed me out and
we parted ways. He went out there and
got on some heavy stuff. This wasn't
something that he did that often.

**I assume this stuff wasn't coming from a
proper doctor right?**
I don't know where he was getting it
from, not that kind of thing anyway.
Elvis called me everything imaginable
and another doctor went on the next
tour. The new doctor changed the
medicine around that I was giving him
and the stuff that he gave him was a
heavy tranquilliser. The problem was
that it had a side effect that would drop
your blood pressure and last a long,
long time. It could just be a few hours,

or it could last twenty-four hours. Elvis
just couldn't wake up. He'd go out there
and he was still groggy and half asleep.
He couldn't do his shows and he
couldn't move.

Did the Colonel or Vernon intervene?
The Colonel and I were not real close but
he called me and asked if I could rejoin
the tour because things had gotten all
screwed up. I said that I wasn't going to
but if Elvis wants to call me to take back
the things he said, then I might consider
it, I just didn't know.

Elvis did another bad show that
night, so the Colonel called me again
and told me that I had to go back
because the shows were getting terrible.
Elvis was screwing things up, he
couldn't remember what he was doing on
stage. The Colonel said that they needed
me to go back and figure out what was
going on.

So, Elvis did finally call and he told
me he was sorry for what had happened.
He asked if I'd go back, so I did. I found
out that if he didn't use that particular
drug, there was no problem with the
shows. This was the only time, as far as
I know, when he'd have such problems
on stage.

I really wanted to quit because my
family was on my butt because I wasn't
at home. My regular patients were on
my butt saying that I was taking care of
Elvis and not taking care of them.

**So, you went back on tour with Elvis, to
sort out the others doctors damage.**
You know, when Elvis was in the
hospital he did well. He got all the
attention he wanted. The only thing he
didn't get was the drugs because
everything had to go through the nurses
at the hospital. I decided that we needed
to do this when he was at home too, so I
told Elvis that I wasn't going to give him
medication through other people and
that I was going to keep his medicine.
We then moved a nurse into Graceland
telling Elvis she was there to look after
his grandma. If Elvis needed something

during the night, the protocol was left with her. I never left anything with him.

Did you ever come across anything given to Elvis by the feel-good doctors in Vegas or Los Angeles?
There was only one good thing that I learned through going to Elvis' house one time. I'd gone up to the bathroom to collect something that he'd left up there next to the sink. I found three bottles of pills, a thousand pills in each bottle. There were uppers, amphetamines, valium and codeine.

When I threw those pills away Elvis got pissed off. I disposed of them right down the commode. Just think how hard it is to treat a grown man just like a child. You needed to be there to give him medicine when he needed it. He was an adult and he should have been able to read the label himself. It took a long time for him to buy that.

Would you say that part of the problem was Elvis' addictive personality?
Oh yeah, there was one time when Elvis came back from California and was almost dead. We took him straight from his plane to the hospital. Another doctor out in California was giving him shots of Demerol, which is a painkiller. His body had gone into shock and I had to detoxify him in the hospital.

If there were such signs of polypharmacy (a drug cocktail), why wasn't he admitted more often?
I admitted him several times into the hospital and the term polypharmacy means nothing. You take any cancer patient walking the street, almost any patient of any kind with a major disease; and they take six, eight, ten medications.

But Elvis' dosages were getting larger because he was becoming immune to the effects.
No, I can't think of one drug where this would be a problem. Let me give you an example. His usage was heaviest when he was on the road because things were

more important to him than at any other time with the shows. He was afraid that if he didn't sleep he wouldn't do a good show. He would come home off the tours and he may go a week, ten days, two weeks without taking a thing. If he was addicted, he couldn't do that. So, I don't think he was immune to anything.

You're saying that Elvis was in control of his intake?
No, he wasn't in control, we were. When you're addicted to something you don't have any say so, you've got to have that drug. It's not something that you've got any mental control over. It's kind of confusing but yes, Elvis had an addictive personality, he would've loved it if somebody was there giving him something all the time.

It must have got to the point where Elvis realised that he was in some kind of danger health wise.
Yeah, he did. But when you need something, you can't rationalise. I tried to get him to go to a clinic but back in those days there weren't many around. I could only find one and that was in Arkansas.

We hear about a whole series of drugs being given to Elvis before and after each and every show.
Well, that's true. Elvis had a lot of trouble with arthritis and he could also suffer from a lot of disc trouble in his back and neck. We could actually predict that if he did a certain number on stage, then he'd hurt like hell afterwards. You know, he'd be snapping his neck around and doing a lot of gyrations. Doing a lot of karate stuff with his bad back. We'd have to treat all that just like any other series of sport injuries.

You'd honestly say that everything you ever prescribed Elvis yourself was needed, nothing extra?
Yes, the only thing that wasn't needed was placebos.

And they are?
The easiest way to make up a placebo is to break open a capsule, take the medicine out and put sugar in it, or salt, instead of the medication. So, that's the way we got around it. Otherwise, everything was given for a reason.

Can you tell me a little about the racquetball venture?
We got Elvis involved in racquetball because we were trying to build up some courts in the United States, we were trying to use his name. Elvis didn't put any money into it, he just agreed for us to use his name. His daddy wasn't happy with the whole thing from the beginning because he didn't know about it. It was the only business venture that Elvis got into that his father didn't have anything to do with. Vernon was not a businessman by any stretch of the imagination. So, one of the guys involved out in Palm Springs somehow found out that one of the other guys who ran the business part of it was getting paid and had got himself car. The rest of us knew nothing about it. Well, he told Elvis about it, he didn't mention it to us, and so Elvis thought we were pulling something behind his back. His daddy found out about it and told him to get out of the deal.

So, Elvis never loaned you any money regarding the racquetball deal?
He put in around $100,000.00 at the very end of it because there were a lot of bills that occurred through him pulling out, a lot of bills that we wouldn't have had if he had stayed there.

Can we lift the mood a little by you telling me your fondest memory of Elvis?
That may've been the time Elvis shot me (laughs). His daddy had just been discharged from the hospital after having a heart attack. Elvis had made a trip out to the dentist's office and he'd asked him for some painkillers. He must've taken a couple of grocery sacks

full. I told him that he wasn't going to have them so he started firing the gun. It was a wonder that his daddy didn't have another heart attack. A bullet bounced off something in the room and I got burned across my chest.

That sounds pretty terrifying. I bet you were worried there for a second.
Not as worried as Elvis was (laughs).

I know all you guys got along great, any other stories from on the road?
We scared the shit out of one of the guys one time. We gave him some red dye in a candy bar he was eating and when he urinated he thought he was dying, it was blood red. I was sitting there when he came in saying that he didn't want to flush the toilet until I'd seen what had happened. I told him to hang on until I'd finished on the phone, but I wasn't actually talking to anybody. He walked back and forth waiting. We had set him up by telling him that this was the way Felton Jarvis had gotten sick, by his urine going red, and he eventually lost his kidneys.

You weren't too cruel to each other then! You have a funny story from New Year's Eve 1975 in Pontiac right?
You know, Elvis was so nervous that night. It was so cold that he was afraid his throat wasn't going to hold up. What with the weather and everything that was going on, he insisted that we flew his throat doctor in from Las Vegas.
   I just told him that I had a friend who was a throat doctor and that he'd take a look at him. We got him in to attend to his throat and Elvis never knew a thing about it. He would have killed me.

Just a regular doctor right?
That's right (laughs).

Well, I know your time is precious, thanks so much for meeting up and allowing me to talk openly with you.
A pleasure, no problem.

> ❝I've never ever in my lifetime seen a man as beautiful as Elvis. He had that charisma, that something, that energy around him... that everyone talks about but you can't put your finger on.❞

Sherry Williams

Diane Johnston talks to Elvis' former girlfriend.

Why have you waited until now to speak about your relationship with Elvis?
Well, I spent all those years dedicated to raising my children, it was basically on the back-burner in my mind. It didn't come to the forefront until I was in Palm Springs last summer. I went by the house, which I'd done once or twice before but when I went by this time, there was something present there. I'm a very spiritual person, I believe in some type of life after death and that day Elvis' spirit was sitting in my car when I was there. His presence was so strong that I had to leave; I couldn't stay. That's when everything started happening for me, things kept flowing back into my mind. It all came to surface, memories of the time I spent with him, and it hasn't left. He has been present in my daily life every day since then, it's like he made himself present to me; he grabbed ahold and hasn't let go since.

It all started when I was parked in front of the Chino Canyon house and since then it's been a unique experience. I've never had anything like that happen to me before.

The other reason is because it was so close and personal to me. I never shared my Elvis life with anyone but my mother and one of my close friends. Recently I've heard so many negative things about how he was, and some people seem to be capitalising on the negativity. My personal relationship with Elvis, and how he was with me, was so positive and I want to share that.

You told me before that it was a friend that introduced you to Elvis back in 1970?
Yes, September 9th, my eighteenth birthday! I turned eighteen in his presence; he didn't know that at the time. It was after the concert in Phoenix up in the hotel room and we stayed until after midnight, turning eighteen while I was there. My friend had met him and asked me a few times to go with her but I had never wanted to go because I wasn't a fan of his, I was more interested in the Beatles. On this occasion she kind of coerced me and said it was for my birthday, but I suspect she just didn't want to go to Phoenix by herself as we lived in LA.

How did you know that Elvis had taken an interest in you?
He kept looking at me. I could tell because he would be talking to someone and glancing at me out of the corner of his eye. I could tell then that there was some kind of connection.

Your first impression?
Gorgeous! I've never ever in my lifetime seen a man as beautiful as he was. He had that charisma, that something, that energy around him... that everyone talks about but you can't put your finger on. He always had it; it was always around him. I've never felt that from any other person again. Everyone who ever met him felt it, but no one can describe what it was.

What happened next?
Before the evening ended Jerry Schilling slipped me a card, which I still have today, that had a telephone number on which to contact Elvis. I never used it.

About a month and a half later the same girlfriend called me and said she'd gotten a call from Charlie [Hodge] inviting her to Palm Springs and asking if she'd bring the same girl that was in Phoenix.

I stayed at the house a couple of days, sleeping on the couch, then went back around November and again in January. Joe [Esposito] told me Elvis wanted me to come to Vegas and I spent most of February 1971 with him there.

Elvis was still married to Priscilla at this time, how did you feel about that?
When Priscilla came to town I'd stay on the 29th floor. I had very mixed feelings about it, very confusing for a sheltered eighteen-year-old girl. If it wasn't me, it was going to be somebody else, so I rationalised it. I had to either accept that or not be there. It was a very complex relationship that I had with him, he was a lot of things to me; a friend, a brother, a father, he wasn't a lover yet (laughs), he played a lot of different roles in my life. There were no male role models in my life; he filled a lot of shoes. He and I talked about that a lot.

And the other women?
I never knew about that at the beginning. I found out only recently that there were others during that same time. I was always led to believe that it was Priscilla in town, when I stayed in the suite below. I was very naive. But, you know, that was Elvis. I don't begrudge him for that! If anybody could get away with it, it was Elvis! (laughs).

Did you get along with the guys?
I never spoke to them very much; I was very shy and introverted. I was very intimidated around these men that were nearly twice my age. Charlie and Joe were very good to me. Ricky Stanley was there a lot and he was closer to my age. Other than that I didn't really communicate with them a lot. It was overwhelming for me. I later learned from one of the guys that Elvis didn't like them talking with his girlfriends. It wasn't allowed.

Did you ever meet the Colonel?
Yes, twice. Both times in Las Vegas. First time that February and the second time either that August or the following February, I don't recall which. On one of those occasions he came up to the suite and he was really angry, he was steamin'. He stormed into the bedroom and told Elvis that many people in the audience had walked out of the show. He was in there about fifteen minutes and then stomped back out. Elvis asked me what I'd thought about the show. It was one of those shows where his antics were hilarious! Elvis was making a lot of 'inside' jokes, which I understood, and I was laughing but you really had to have known him to get the jokes - a real *inside* show. I thought it was really funny but I could see where people in the audience were not happy with it as there was more joking around than there was singing. I got the impression that the Colonel had slapped his wrist, so to speak. Elvis was very subdued after that. There was no party in the suite that night!

So was the next show any different as a result of the Colonel's visit?
Oh yeah, very different. Back to work.

In my opinion it was probably one of the better shows he'd ever done after that happened.

Is that show the most memorable to you?
I couldn't tell you how many shows I saw, over fifty, and there's no certain one. More individual songs than one entire show. I remember when he sang *Just Pretend* and pointed over at the booth where I was, that was a favourite song that meant something to me.

Any other special songs?
Yes, the other special one for me is *Until It's Time For You To Go.* My favourite song from way back is *Don't.* In Palm Springs one night I was sleeping on the couch Elvis came out with this flashlight to see if I was sleeping. I had been sleeping until he shone the light in my face (laughs) and he just sat down beside me and he whispered some of the lyrics gently in my ear. I had told him earlier in the day what a beautiful song it was.

You visited Graceland?
Yes, he took me to Graceland in 1974; that was really special. I hadn't seen Elvis for about a year when out of the blue they called me to go to Palm Springs. They said Linda [Thompson] was there and Elvis wanted me to join the group. While in Palm Springs he asked me to go to Graceland for a week. I wondered, 'What's this all about?' I didn't realise that Elvis was seeing other women when he was with Linda, he wasn't monogamous when he was with Priscilla so why would I think he was with Linda? But I did. I stayed in Memphis for a week and we did a lot of things, theatre, karate, shopping etc. I kept wondering 'why am I here?'.

When I went to leave, Elvis called me aside and asked me to stay a couple of days because Linda was going shopping or off with a girlfriend for a few days. It wasn't in a romantic way, we spent most

of the time upstairs reading books and talking. Basically, I think he wanted someone to stay with him while she was gone. However, it was one of the more intimate times I had with him.

Elvis wanted to buy you a car, but you refused?
Yes, that's not what our relationship was about, even though he was a very generous man. I was happy to be around him, he was such an energetic person, I had so much fun when I was with him. It was so exciting for me, this little girl from high school. They were the most amazing years my life to this day, except having my children.

In Memphis he went on this great spree, buying cars for everybody. But I had just bought myself a little Datsun 240Z sports car that was only six

" I wanted to live the life of someone my age and when I was with Elvis I wasn't. I was missing out on my own life. Elvis' lifestyle wasn't my lifestyle. I wanted to experience what 18, 19, 20 year old girls experience. "

months old. I told him I didn't need one, want one, how would I get it back to LA? I kept coming up with excuses because I loved my car and waited a long time to buy it. I talked him out of it and he asked me how much it was and I think I'd owed about $3000 on it.

When we returned to Graceland he called me up to his office and when I get there he's got handfuls of $100 bills. He counted out thirty of them and handed them to me to pay for the car. I cried; I was so touched. He insisted I take it and so I paid for my car. He gave me many other things including jewellery and my TLC necklace, which he gave me in February 1971. That was the most special thing to me; I wear it often to this day.

You previously told me the interesting secret to Elvis' soft lips, would you like to share that with our female readers?
Elvis had the most soft, sensual lips that I've ever kissed. He'd use A&D ointment on his lips all the time, probably every hour (laughs), every time he went past the bathroom or into the bedroom. He used that as much as he used the Colgate toothpaste, and it had to be Colgate, at least in the early '70s.

We'd kiss so passionately that I'd get the worst razor burn on my cheeks, it hurt so much but I loved it 'cause I knew where it was from (laughs). My face was just so sensitive. I'd use the A&D on my chipmunk cheeks too, to help the sting from his shaven beard. He had the softest lips - I had the softest cheeks!

When did your relationship break up?
There was no big break up because I never really felt like I was a girlfriend. Eventually we did have a physical relationship for some time but it was a different role than a girlfriend. He encompassed so many different roles in my life.

I didn't feel old enough to be a girlfriend. We stopped spending time together during 1972. We saw each other a couple of times during 1973 and then that week in 1974. I wanted to live the life of someone my age and when I was with Elvis I wasn't. I was missing out on my own life. I didn't see any future in it, didn't even know if I wanted any future in it. His lifestyle wasn't my lifestyle. I wanted to experience what 18, 19, 20-year-old girls experience. I jumped straight from high school into the Elvis world and I didn't want to miss my own life... does that make sense? I saw my friends doing things that I wanted to do. Time went on and I met my husband in 1975 and got married in 1976.

When was the last time you actually saw Elvis?
I saw him briefly in Hawaii in 1977. I was on vacation and we talked for about 30 or 40 minutes.

What did you talk about?
We talked in general about his tour, about how he was feeling, about what he was doing, what I was doing. I did not tell him I'd married, I remember making the decision not to tell him that. I don't know why, I think in the back of my mind, I knew that once someone had gotten married Elvis never really

involved himself with them any more.

I'm not sure I was ready for a closure like that. I didn't want that finality, that ending.

Did Elvis mention the book *Elvis: What Happened?*

Elvis looked at me and said, "Baby, they wrote a book." I said, "I know." I knew of course he was referring to *Elvis: What Happened?* He looked out over the ocean; his eyes were so lost in thought and had such a far away look. Nothing more needed to be said, his eyes said it all.

He looked much different to me, obviously more overweight than when I'd seen him in 1974, but I did not realise the danger he was in. I didn't recognise it, I don't know that it would've made any difference. Probably not, but it still bothered me, that I didn't recognise it. That was the last time I saw him.

When I returned to the hotel I said to my husband, "I'll be surprised if he lives another six months." But I did not mean it, literally. I said it because of his weight, kind of flippant; I really didn't mean anything by it. To this day I wonder why that came from my mouth.

Do you have a special story that you can share with our readers?

Once Elvis kept asking me to join him and a few guests at the piano to sing gospel songs with them.

I really did not want to do this, as I can't sing a note. Not only that, but I can't even begin to carry a tune.

I told Elvis this, practically pleading with him. Of course, he would not hear of it. "Come over here next to me baby, just sing along with us." I hesitated and told him he'd be sorry. I had sung only a few notes, when he looked at me... stopped... and looked at me again. He stopped playing, started with his infamous grin and just started laughing. "You weren't kiddin' were you honey?" and he laughed himself right off the piano bench onto the floor. I was

laughing with him and was not at all embarrassed or offended. I had warned him and I knew that I was tone deaf. "It's OK boys, she makes up for it in other ways... Oh, Lord have mercy!" he said laughing. I was embarrassed with that remark! From then on I just continued to sit quietly next to him at the piano. Needless to say, I never tried it again, and he didn't ask!

Anything you'd like to add Sherry?

What a wonderful man he was. Anyone whose life he touched is the better for it. I feel so privileged that it was during such great time in his life. When I see the shows from 1970 to 1972 to me they're like watching home movies and to be part of that is so special to me.

I still miss him but will always have the memories. He really affected my life a lot. That's such an impressionable age and he exposed me to a lot of things I otherwise would never have experienced had I not met him. He was a huge impact on my life, in a spiritual way too. All positive and fun, nothing he ever said or did was negative towards me in any way. I was very sheltered naïve eighteen year old and he could've had an impact that affected me in an adverse way but he was very intuitive to that and was very aware of that. I think that's why he sheltered me from a lot of things that could've affected me in a negative way. Or he could've chosen not to have me be a part of his life in any way, but I'm glad he did (laughs).

I never saw any of the terrible anger or drug taking that many people talk about. I'm not saying it didn't happen, I'm just saying I didn't see it. He would take two Placidyl in bed to go to sleep and I took a smaller one, as it was hard for me get to sleep during the day. Other than that, I never saw Elvis taking any drugs. He never offered me anything, I never saw him take anything. I hear all these stories but that wasn't anything that I was ever part of. Remember though, this was very early '70s. I remember twice I missed his show and stayed in his suite due to headaches and he gave me Excedrin [over the counter medicine] for it, he never gave me anything else despite there being ample opportunity.

As I said, I wasn't a fan prior to meeting Elvis. To this day I've only seen five of his movies! The music I like is what he did at the time I was around him. The reason I was originally attracted to Elvis was because he was the most beautiful man I'd ever seen in my life, didn't matter what his age was. He was very young at heart also, kind of at my level when having fun. He did such silly things that made him seem younger than his age, and of course he didn't look thirty-five. The parts of being Elvis didn't really entice me because I didn't know his music too well. Obviously I knew who he was, but wasn't a fan. When I went to Palm Springs the first time he got a real kick out of the fact that, at that time, I'd only seen one movie. He made a big deal to Charlie "Can you believe it, Sherry has seen only one movie!" The third time I went to Palm Springs was on the 9th January and I didn't know it had been his birthday the previous day. He couldn't believe there was someone in his house that didn't know it had just been his birthday. It was unheard of that there would be someone there that didn't know it had been his birthday the day before. I think he liked that about me, I was someone who didn't know everything about him. Elvis wasn't used to that, and I think it attracted him. I feel very fortunate that I got to spend the times with Elvis that were so very positive for him. It was during the good times of his life. It hurts me that people tend to focus on the later years, his troubled years. We all have troubled times in our lives. Lets focus on the good times; most of his years were good years. Maybe that's why he was sitting in my car that day in Palm Springs, maybe he got tired of hearing all the negativity too!

I didn't even know this whole Elvis world existed out there. I'm amazed and thrilled for him that it does. I knew Graceland was open but I didn't know anything about what was going on, I had no idea!

I visited Graceland recently for the first time since 1974; it was extremely hard for me. Joe [Esposito] had arranged for Patsy [Andersen] to be with me, as I couldn't do it on my own. She was really great. I spent a few hours at the house but I couldn't really hold up at the Meditation Garden so I'm going to return sometime this year.

Sherry, thank you for sharing your incredible memories with us. I'm looking forward to seeing you at *The New Gladiator Reunion* in Memphis this August.
You're welcome. It's been a pleasure. I've sent a tube of A&D ointment for you. I look forward to seeing you in August too.

"If you've got somebody telling you to go for it at a young age, then your dreams will come true."

Suzanna Leigh

In the summer of 1965 Elvis returned to the beautiful Island of Hawaii to make his twenty-first feature film. He was cast as Rick Richards, a struggling pilot who sets up a charter service with his friend Danny Kohana (James Shigeta).

Starring along side him was an attractive twenty-year-old British actress named Suzanna Leigh who was cast in the main female role as Judy Hudson, a secretary employed by the firm. Rick soon fell for Judy and along with some memorable scenery and another Presley film became a classic.

The career of Suzanna Leigh stretches way back to 1960. Her list of achievements is very impressive with twenty-six movies and endless TV programmes to her credit. She has worked with such legends as Tony Curtis and Jerry Lewis, but her most documented movie is still the much-loved *Paradise, Hawaiian Style*.

We have been extremely lucky to be able to talk to Suzanna. She openly spoke about her days with Elvis and their unique friendship. Since 1980 she has been extremely busy raising her daughter Natalia and releasing her autobiography. Since making *Paradise, Hawaiian Style*, Elvis has stayed very much in her thoughts and to this day Suzanna holds some wonderful memories of filming in the sun with the world's greatest superstar.

Andrew Hearn interviewed the actress who doesn't like to be called baby, not even by Elvis!

When did you first come across Elvis Presley?
My brother, who was a big fan, is ten years older than I am, so I always heard his records. I remember when I was quite young I heard him on the radio, it was a wonderful song called *Old Shep*. As I sat and listened I started to cry because there was a magic in the song. First of all there was that voice and even today there's nothing that comes even close to his talent. There's something about that voice.

How did you feel about landing a part in one of his movies?
It was great. I had already made several movies in Hollywood and Hal Wallis was looking for an English girl to co-star with Elvis. I was very excited to be in the movie.

How long did you guys actually stay in Hawaii filming?
It was a movie that should have taken just fifteen days and for a film that was supposed to be very short just got longer and longer, which was lovely. We actually spent about three months there due to Elvis' love of the island. You see, he had so much power and often he'd tell the director that he didn't feel much like filming and he and I would sneak off to talk. No other Hollywood star would be allowed to act like this but you know Elvis.

Most fans remember the slightly annoying little actress Donna Butterworth.
Well, I didn't have a problem with her but Elvis did! Take a look at the film and you'll spot Elvis looking off camera at me

during certain scenes with her. I remember her being very over-the-top and she really did drive us all scatty. I honestly have no idea what happened to her after the film.

Was that really you flying that plane?
No, unfortunately not, but I quickly became interested and I ended up with a full pilot's licence as a result.

I believe Elvis had a surprise visitor at a hotel in Hawaii?
Could you be referring to the lady in the coat? She seemed just like any other Elvis fan and she was very attractive and sweet. She spent quite some time talking to us and I began to like her very much. One day, whilst talking to Elvis, she wore a long coat, which she allowed to just drop to the floor and she didn't have a stitch on underneath. As she stood there smiling I immediately started to run in embarrassment but Elvis grabbed me and pulled me back. He wasn't going to face her alone and he calmly continued to finish the autograph.

Although there are photographs of you both kissing, I've noticed that you and Elvis didn't actually kiss in the film.
No, but we made up for it afterwards (laughs)! We'd already made the film and eighteen photographers were snapping publicity shots and Elvis just said "Let's do it." So, that's how come there are pictures of us kissing although it didn't quite happen in the film. We were just checking that we were still good friends... somebody had to do it!

There's a part in the film where you get mad at Elvis and call him names, how easy was that?
Well, we were just professional actors doing our jobs. I didn't mean it!

What about Elvis' skills at acting?
He was very professional and he was never late on the set. You see, Elvis never went to drama school and I didn't, but his knowledge of Shakespeare was simply amazing. He loved to quote and he always knew better than I did.

So was Elvis' interest in Shakespeare the main topic in-between filming?
After filming we'd scurry off to chat like mad because time was precious. We only made the one film together so we loved to just talk. In fact, Elvis had asked if we could make another movie together called *Easy Come, Easy Go.* Although Hal Wallis wanted to go along with Elvis' request, the Screen Actors Guild refused to allow me to play another American. But yes, our time was spent mainly talking.

Did Elvis talk to you about his mother on these occasions?
His mother and my father thought the world of us both in almost extreme ways and they actually died at the same age. He often said that she would have loved me and that he missed her. My father always encouraged me, and his mother was the same with him. So if you've got somebody telling you to go for it at a young age, then your dreams will come true. Gladys made things happen for Elvis.

Were you the victim of any of the famous Presley pranks?
Elvis mainly kept these jokes for the guys but I did spring a surprise on him during a break in filming. I actually went along to make-up who did a wonderful job in turning me into a very realistic old lady and with a little help from the wardrobe department it was very convincing. Elvis seemed surprised to see this strange person making her way towards him calling his name, I told him I'd managed to sneak past security and I really wanted an autograph and to my amazement, he still didn't recognise me.

Well, any little old English lady who managed to get past the tight security at MGM deserved and autograph and Elvis began to oblige. As he did so I threw back my head making him jump and everyone laughed, including Elvis.

What actually made you close friends?
Elvis had this amazing power. If you met this man and got on with him, you'd want to tell him things that you didn't tell anyone else, and you felt he knew exactly what you were talking about.

I was very happy to be able to talk to him openly because I knew that he cared about me and about what really happened to me when I was a child. We actually spent sixteen hours a day together during the filming of *Paradise, Hawaiian Style* that took months to complete and during this time we became close. He was very kind and a wonderful friend.

Did you see him at all after the movie was completed?
Sadly not. Elvis didn't like to talk much on the phone and I never really saw him in person to talk to, although I sometimes wrote to him at Graceland.

I managed to see his show in Las Vegas in 1972, although I didn't go backstage or anything and he wasn't even aware that I was in the audience, but it was good to see Elvis perform for his fans. I was, and still am, a very big fan and he was fantastic in concert.

Elvis was well-known for being wonderful to his fans wasn't he?
Yes he really was. You know, he always listened to the radio on the set and Elvis actually bought the DJ a Harley Davidson motorbike after hearing him say he'd like to own one. He bought me a Harley that day too, and by the time he'd finished, everyone had one, it was amazing. He kindly gave me a beautiful bracelet that I treasured but sadly, it was stolen from me some time ago. I can also remember two English fans, a mother and daughter I believe, that spent some time just hanging around the set. Everyone was shocked when word got out that the mother had suddenly died of a heart attack and the daughter was understandably in need of help. Elvis became very upset and concerned, he took care of the girl and

actually paid for her mother's body to be flown back to England, that was just Elvis.

What about your new book?
I'd love the fans to support my book, which is not in any way just about Elvis; it's about me. There is obviously a large section about Elvis that is terribly important, as he was such a big part of my life. I have written things that Elvis told me that I've never shared with anyone before and I'm sure the fans will want to read it. I mean, there were things that were very important to him that we both shared, the whole of that religious thing for starters. I had a very keen interest in all kinds of religion, but in the '60s you just didn't talk about those things for fear of being taken away by men in white coats. Once Elvis discovered we had similar interests we talked all the time.

Do you think that because you weren't sexual partners, the book will appeal even more to fans?
Elvis used to say to me that I was the sister he never had and I felt the same way about him as my brother and I didn't get on. Perhaps we became such good friends that Elvis told me things he may not have told others and if an affair had taken place this might not have been the case.

Do you have any more unpublished photographs like the ones in the book?
I do have half a film of wonderful snaps that Elvis organised and as far as I can remember, he took the other half. They are beautiful colour pictures of Elvis and I just in the sunshine. Yes, I do own some fantastic photographs that will please any fan.

Well, thanks Suzanna for taking time to talk to me about your time with Elvis.
It's a pleasure and I'd like to say that Elvis was the most wonderful man I had ever worked with, and I will always treasure the fond memories.

"It was very easy to work with Elvis because he was so friendly. We just sat around the piano and did a few songs. It was fun."

Glen D. Hardin

Glen D. Hardin was a member of Elvis' band from 1970 to 1976, and was also responsible for many musical arrangements for the shows. He also toured with the likes of Emmylou Harris for three years, John Denver for sixteen years, and with Buddy Holly's original Crickets for eleven.

As one of the hottest piano players around, Glen has worked as an arranger and recording session musician with stars like Merle Haggard, Marty Robbins, Dolly Parton, Tanya Tucker, the Everly Brothers, Willie Nelson, Bing Crosby, Andy Williams, Dean Martin, Sammy Davis Jr., Sonny & Cher, Roy Orbison and Tina Turner. Andrew Hearn caught up with Glen at his home in Nashville to find out more about his years on the road with Elvis.

Glen, can you tell us where you were born and how you got into music?
I was born in Collinsworth County, Texas in 1939, or was it 1839? I played around a little here and there like everybody did back then, but went to Los Angeles in 1961 and I got shot at a nightclub out there in '62. Soon after that I joined the Crickets and got lucky playing on sessions and things.

Do you still tour with the Crickets?
I do once in a while, yeah.

Can you ever remember hearing Elvis on the radio back in the '50s?
I first heard him in '54 there in Texas, and I liked him a lot.

Did you ever see him live back then?
I did, yeah. He came to where I lived in Texas three times, and I think I saw him all three times.

Can you remember when you very first got to meet Elvis?
It was in 1970, I guess, just before I went over to work for him. I went over to audition for him, but I already knew everybody in the band and they wanted me with them. It was very easy because he was so friendly. We just sat around the piano and did a few songs. It was fun.

Where did this take place?
It was in LA at MGM, although it may've been at RCA, I can't quite remember where it was.

We know that Larry Muhoberac was Elvis piano player during those first comeback shows in '69, but I assume James Burton asked you first, right?
He did, although Larry had worked with Elvis before, I think it was on some records in Memphis, so I'm really not 100% sure that I would've got the job, Larry may've already had it. He did it for that first time, then for reasons of his own he just didn't want to do it anymore because he wanted to stay in Los Angeles.

Was that to carry on with his session work?
Yeah.

Have you any idea why Elvis and the band rehearsed so many songs but only

the same few were used in the show over so many years?
Firstly, we rehearsed so many songs because Elvis just liked to get together and just hang out for the most part and, of course, whilst we were at it we got a lot of work done. The idea being to touch on as many songs as anyone could remember just in case he ever wanted to do them on stage.

Can you remember how Elvis dressed at these rehearsals? Was he still very flamboyant?
Well, a little bit, but he was still pretty casual.

Elvis made some of his shows memorable because of his improvisation, plus, you guys never really knew what he was going to do next did you?
Yeah, that's right.

Did he ever have you stumped by a particular song or something that he did?
Not really. We all did very well with that and I think that everybody knew what he was all about.

Did he ever pull any pranks on you whilst on stage?
He joked with the band all the time, but nothing in particular that I can remember. Just things like not sticking to the list, you know? He might just go into something new maybe.

It's always surprised me that nobody on stage ever got an electric shock with all the water Elvis threw at you guys. Is that why Elvis stood fairly still during the *Aloha from Hawaii* show in '73?
No, I really don't know. But if I remember correctly the stage was kind of small and there wasn't much room up there for him to move around.

Did you feel nervous about that particular show?
No, not really because we shot it at 2:30 in the morning and it seemed like it had

been a long day and so we really wanted to get up there and do it, and then go home. We enjoyed it very much, and I'll never forget it.

What do you recall of the dreaded 1975 New Year's Eve show on Pontiac?
That was one of the very last live concerts that I ever played with Elvis and I thought it was terrible. It was freezing cold too. In fact, I can't tell you how cold it was. But in March I went to Memphis and played part of an album with him.

So, what were those last sessions at Graceland like?
They just took forever, Elvis never showed up until late. In fact, he showed up on Thursday, and we'd all been waiting there since Sunday. The whole session was dreadfully slow and very tiring.

What was his mood like at these sessions?
He might've had something on his mind, so he'd sing just a little bit at at time, but he really didn't get with it.

Were any of you guys aware of Elvis' drug usage at the time?
We all know he was on something because we'd see him before a show and doubt that we was going to be able to make it, then all of a sudden he'd just come out wired.

Did you mix much with Elvis off stage?
Oh, an awful lot, especially in his suite in Vegas.

Jerry Scheff told me that you both went up to Elvis' house in LA and Priscilla cooked you chilli. Do you remember that incident?
Oh yeah, we all lived in LA at the time and he invited us over constantly to his house there, or to Palm Springs. Wherever it was, we were always welcome. I'm not sure who went that day, I think it was all of us, but he

called and invited us and we went over to eat. We just sat around having a good time.

Do you remember when Elvis gave you your TCB necklace?
Sure I do. I guess it was about 1970 and all the others got theirs at the same time. I still have it. I don't wear it all that much, but I would never sell it.

Did he give you anything else as a special gift?
He gave me rings, watches... he gave everybody gifts at the same time, although we all got something different. We all got something together, not always, but most of the time.

What's your fondest memory of Elvis, either on or off stage? Is there a particular incident that sticks in your mind the most?
There are so many memories that it's really hard to say. We just had a really good time. It was always very casual and always a lot of fun. It'd be almost impossible to try and pick just one memory.

When Elvis died, where you shocked, or did you see the end coming?
He was in bad health, and we all knew that, but I don't think we knew it was all that bad because I was shocked. In a way I was surprised, but in another I wasn't. I know it sounds silly but I

guess you're always shocked when someone dies.

Did he ever express a concern about his health or appearance to you?
Not to me, but I think he did to others. I think that it did worry him.

Moving on to *Elvis - The Concert*. Was that first big 1997 show in Memphis quite emotional for you guys as Elvis wasn't there?
Well, it was in a way. You've got to remember that we rehearsed a lot but there was still a great deal to remember, so I just cleared my mind and got on with the show. I didn't have time to think about much. It was a very big audience and all of that, but we were ready.

At that point, how long had it been since the band had last seen one another?
It had been a while, but the guys and I had always been in touch and once in a while we'd work together on a project or something. I hadn't seen the Stamps or The Sweet Inspirations in many years.

Did you find yourselves talking about the old times touring with Elvis?
Oh yeah, very much, and we were all overjoyed when they wanted to put us on the road again. At first, I didn't think it would be a very good show, but of course, I was pleasantly surprised, especially with how it's been received around the world. So, Memphis was a very good starting place.

Why are a few band members missing like Kathy Westmoreland and John Wilkinson?
I don't really get involved with that side of the organisation, but I suspect that the book Kathy wrote may've been at odds with Graceland, but I don't know that for sure. John Wilkinson had a stroke and that's the reason he's not there. I know that Charlie [Hodge] was not invited back after that first show in Memphis.

Are the other guys as happy with its continued success, or are they getting tired of it?
We're not tired of doing it because it's such a good show, and any time that you're part of something good that the audience likes, it makes it very enjoyable. It's a lot of good music and it goes real quick when you're sitting up there on that stage. It doesn't seem like you're up there more than twenty minutes because it's so tight. But it's still a lot of fun to play.

Last time we spoke you told me that whenever Elvis got on the piano you cringed. Was he really that bad?
I thought that he was terrible on the piano.

Do you remember any of the times when he threw you off your seat to play something himself on stage?
Yeah, he was doing it towards the end of the time that I toured with him. Right in the middle of the show, he'd just come over and ask me to hold the microphone for him. He'd then just sit down and sing whilst I held his microphone.

Before we close, I'd like to ask you how the world should remember Elvis Presley.
For the singer that he was, and for his contribution to music.

Fantastic! It's been a thrill and a pleasure being able to talk to you again Glen, and I'd like to thank you for your time.
Keep sending those magazines, I really enjoy them.

Guide to Illustrations

Cover photo: Publicity still for *Loving You* - Spring 1957 © Tom Salva

Page 11: With John Wilkinson in Las Vegas - August 23, 1973
Page 13: Publicity still for *Jailhouse Rock* - 1957
Page 15: With Julie Parrish on set of *Paradise, Hawaiian Style* - August 1965
Page 17: With Julie Parrish on set of *Paradise, Hawaiian Style* - August 1965
Page 18: With Mike Stoller and Jerry Leiber at MGM Studios - Spring 1957
Page 20: Publicity still for *Love Me Tender* - 1956
Page 21: Publicity still for *Love Me Tender* - 1956
Page 22: With Jennifer Holden in *Jailhouse Rock* - May 1957
Page 24: With Jennifer Holden in *Jailhouse Rock* - May 1957
Page 25: With *Jailhouse Rock* co-stars Judy Tyler and Jennifer Holden - 1957
Page 27: With Lamar Fike on leave in Paris - June 1957
Page 30: Publicity still for *Loving You* - Spring 1957
Page 31: Publicity still for *Loving You* - Spring 1957
Page 32: With Jimmy Saville on the set of *Roustabout* - March 1964
Page 33: With Jimmy Saville on the set of *Wild in the Country* - Autumn 1960
Page 35: Tamara Beckwith © Tamara Beckwith
Page 37: Backstage at the Houston Astrodome, Texas - February 28, 1970
Page 38: Al Dvorin in the United Kingdom - August 1999
Page 40: With Francine York (centre) in *Tickle Me* - Autumn 1964
Page 42: On the set of *Roustabout* - March 1964
Page 43: On the set of *Harum Scarum* - March 1965
Page 44: Boarding the Lisa Marie airplane - Summer 1976
Page 47: On the set of *Flaming Star* - August 1960
Page 48: During the *Wild in the Country* sessions - November 1960
Page 50: With Deborah Walley on the set of *Spinout* - Spring 1966
Page 55: *That's The Way It Is* rehearsals in Culver City, California - July 15, 1970
Page 57: *That's The Way It Is* rehearsals in Culver City, California - July 15, 1970
Page 58: With Sonny West during rehearsals in Culver City, California - August 4, 1970
Page 63: At Sonny West's Memphis wedding - December 28, 1970
Page 67: At Los Angeles airport - January 6, 1970
Page 71: Relaxing in Las Vegas - August 1969
Page 75: With Anita Wood in Memphis - 1956
Page 76: Shooting the *Guitar Man* sequence in Burbank, California - June 1968
Page 79: Publicity still for *Loving You* - Spring 1957
Page 81: *That's The Way It Is* rehearsals in Culver City, California - July 15, 1970
Page 82: With Linda Thompson - 1974
Page 84: With Linda Thompson's brother Sam and his wife Louise in Las Vegas - November 1975
Page 87: Boarding the Lisa Marie with Linda Thompson - Long Beach, Cal. April 26, 1976
Page 88: Linda Thompson today © Linda Thompson
Page 90: Barbara Leigh - Early 1970s © Barbara Leigh
Page 95: Performing in Miami Beach, Florida - September 12, 1970
Page 97: Barbara Leigh - Early 1970s © Barbara Leigh
Page 99: Posing with a large teddy bear in Las Vegas - May 1956
Page 100: With Wink Martindale on his *Dance Party* TV show - June 16, 1956
Page 103: Marsha Alverson meets Elvis in Huntsville, Alabama - May 31, 1975 © Keith Alverson
Page 105: Keith Alverson meets Elvis in Huntsville, Alabama - May 31, 1975 © Keith Alverson
Page 106: With Pat Priest in *Easy Come, Easy Go* - Autumn 1966

Whilst every care has been taken with this book and Essential Elvis magazine, the publisher / author does not accept any liability for inaccuracies. Opinions expressed are not necessarily those of the author unless stated.

Special thanks to www.elvisnews.com, Elvis Unlimited, Sara Erwin, Andylon Lensen, Willem Kaauw, Julie Mundy, David Wilson, Diane Johnston, Andrea Virgo and all our friends and staff for their help.

We are grateful to all the suppliers of Elvis photographs used. Every effort has been made to trace the original owner of each photograph, but in some cases this hasn't been possible. Thanks to Russ Howe, Joe Tunzi, Sean Shaver, Jim Hannaford, Bob Heis, Keith Alverson, Ed Bonja, Paul Lichter, Len and Rosemary Leech, Jim Curtin, Tom Salva, Bud Glass, Maria Columbus, Sandi Miller, Robin Rosaaen, Flaming Star magazine and anyone we may not have been able to contact.

We are especially grateful to Russ Howe and Keith Alverson for their contributions to this book. Russ Howe's outstanding collection of photos can be viewed on his website **www.kingcandids.com** and you can email Keith Alverson at **eponstage@charter.net** for details on how to purchase his stunning photographs.

Copyright © Essential Elvis UK 2005. Do not borrow without permission

essential elvis

Why not subscribe to the most talked about Elvis Presley publication?

Our exciting 40-page glossy magazine will keep you right up to date with all the latest Elvis news from around the world

We guarantee our readers more exclusive interviews illustrated with many rare and unreleased photos, well written and honest reviews along with great features

As a company we enjoy full support and regular contributions from Sony / BMG / FTD.

This enables us to offer our subscribers the latest products, at competitive prices.

We are a worldwide publication, officially recognised and commended by EPE

Packed with informative news...
Pages of unreleased photos...
It's refreshing and modern...
Always entertaining...

Subscribing couldn't be easier. The annual fee quoted entitles you to six bumper issues distributed to your door bi-monthly. There are several ways to submit your details...

UK **£15.00**
Europe **£20.00**
Rest of World **£23.00**

American fans may send $30.00 directly to our US office in Memphis
PO Box 161334, Memphis, Tenn. 38186

We accept cash (registered) / cheques POs / IMOs / and all major credit cards

Send to: Essential Elvis. PO Box 4176 Worthing, W. Sussex BN14 9DW, UK

For an instant subscription please call and quote your credit / debit card details on **(+44) (0)1903 525917**

You can now subscribe safely online at **www.essentialelvis.com**

Other exclusive interviews which have appeared in Essential Elvis magazine include...

Sir Cliff Richard
Nancy Sinatra
Vinnie Jones
Wayne Carman
Frank Tarver
Marty Pasetta
Myrna Smith
Reggie Young
Ross Hagen
Mamie Van Doren
JD Sumner
Marty Lacker
Peter Noone
Lew Allen
Jerry Schilling
Joe Esposito
Sam Thompson
Steve Binder
Shirley Dieu
Richard Davis
Paul Evans
Kang Rhee
Dr. Joel M. Cook
Nancy Rooks
Joseph Tunzi
Norman Rossington
Patsy Andersen
Lowell Hays
Bud Glass
Dave Hebler

essential elvis

Join us online by visiting our website at **www.essentialelvis.com**

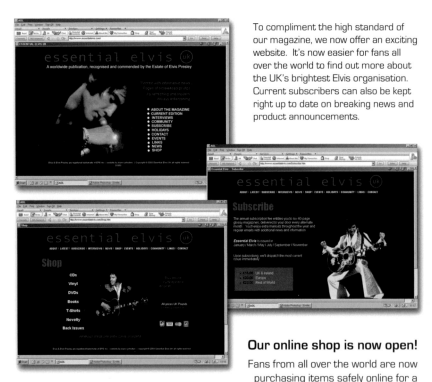

To compliment the high standard of our magazine, we now offer an exciting website. It's now easier for fans all over the world to find out more about the UK's brightest Elvis organisation. Current subscribers can also be kept right up to date on breaking news and product announcements.

Our online shop is now open!

Fans from all over the world are now purchasing items safely online for a quick delivery. We offer a fantastic selection of Elvis memorabilia including vinyl, DVDs, T-shirts, novelty items and a complete catalogue of BMG and Follow That Dream titles.

Please subscribe to our online newsletter, designed to ensure that information and product news reaches you promptly.

- **Breaking news**
- **Online Elvis shop**
- **Mailouts**
- **Chatroom**
- **Messageboard**
- **Information**